The Burning Cedars

Volume 1

THE BEGINNING

RAMZY BAROODY

The Burning Cedars

THE BURNING CEDARS

A PERSONAL ACCOUNT OF A BOY'S LIFE JOURNEY THROUGH THE LEBANESE CIVIL WAR

RAMZY BAROODY

www.TheBurningCedars.com

RAMZY BAROODY

Copyright © 2012 Ramzy Baroody
All rights reserved.
ISBN-13: 9780615647661
ISBN-10: 0615647669

The Burning Cedars

RAMZY BAROODY

**OPEN YOUR DOORS,
O LEBANON,
SO THAT FIRE MAY DEVOUR
YOUR CEDARS!**

ZECHARIAH 11:1

The Burning Cedars

On the morning of April 13, 1975, the Lebanese civil war got underway and for the next fifteen years, countless broken agreements and cease fires, un-eventful negotiations, foreign "peace keeping" troops, special envoys, US Marines and warships, Israeli Invasions, Arab League accords, International interventions and shifting alliances, all failed to halt the violent massacres, the cruel bloodshed and the total destruction of my country. Its cause was multifaceted yet its effects clear, deliberate and calculated.

With over 200,000 civilian fatalities, one million wounded, 350,000 displaced and over one million fleeing the country, Lebanon, nicknamed "Switzerland of the East" along with its capital Beirut, "Paris of the Middle East," lay in ruin, powerfully disintegrated and effectively polarized.

RAMZY BAROODY

Among all the ruin and chaos, a small boy and his family miraculously endured and survived to tell their story.

A story of wealth and poverty, of laughter and pain, of holy visions and depression, of sadness and loneliness and of triumph and survival. A family desperately trying to stay alive and stay together against overwhelming odds, hopeless chances and dire circumstances.

I was eleven when the war started yet its effects, memories, sounds and smells will remain forever fixed in my mind. For better or worse, these events and their ensuing effects made me the person I am today.

This is my story of growing up in Lebanon.

The Burning Cedars

CHAPTER ONE

ALEY

I was eleven in 1975 when the Lebanese civil war began. Lebanon was a beautiful country with soaring fertile mountains crashing into the blue Mediterranean Sea, clear fresh air and year-round clement temperature gave the country its nickname "The Paris of the Middle East." Tourists from all over the world flocked into the country to bask in its warm summer sun and ski its commanding slopes in winter.

I grew up in the village of Aley, a picturesque town in Mount Lebanon, 17 km uphill from Beirut. The word "Aley" derivatives from Aramaic, and means "high place," referring to the town's high altitude above sea level. In the late 1800s, Aley gained prominence when the railroad that passed through it was built linking the Lebanese capital of Beirut to the Syrian capital, Damascus. The railroad provided the residents of Beirut easy means of transportation to the mountains, and this made Aley a popular destination to cool off in the summer months and enjoy its pleasant climate.

I rode this train only once when I was a kid and we traveled 30 km (19 miles) to the town of Zahle in the Beqaa valley located 1000 meters above sea level. Towering above the town at an elevation of 2628 meters (8622 feet) is Mount Sannine, which is

The Burning Cedars

dominated by forests of the most renowned symbol of Lebanon, the cedar trees. Those trees go back to biblical times and their timber was prized by the Egyptian Pharos for shipbuilding and Solomon used them in the construction of the first temple of Jerusalem. In 1998, the cedars were added to the UNESCO list of World Heritage Sites and are rigorously protected. Today, the Damascus highway has replaced the train as the major thoroughfare between Beirut and villages and towns to the north all the way to the Syrian Capital.

Lebanon's tourism is the major source of income for the country as wealthy Arabs from the Gulf States escape the sand and heat to enjoy the cool summer temperatures and bustling nightlife, spending their oil money freely on cars, liquor and women.

The climate in Lebanon differs greatly between the year-round warm temperatures of Beirut and the cold and snowy surrounding mountains. We have a saying in Lebanon that one could swim the Mediterranean sea then ski the mountain slopes all in the same day.

My village of Aley enjoyed cool summers and cold snowy winters. The day usually starts out with sunny skies giving way to overcast and cool afternoons as the warm air from the Mediterranean sweeps over Beirut climbing slowly up the steep mountainside then condensing into thick sheets of mist once met by the cool mountain air, forming dense fog and obscuring everything in its path. The cold and wintry season lasts from September to the middle of April. Summers are pleasant and dry and the lack of rain transforms green and lush meadows into overgrown jungles of tall yellow grass.

RAMZY BAROODY

The Burning Cedars

CHAPTER TWO

THE OLD HOUSE

When by grandfather began building our house in the early 1900s, he discovered a natural spring on the premises with its source high up in the mountains miles away. He captured its pure and ice-cold waters in a large underground cement cave-like structure he built that was accessible through a long and dark passageway. Many stray cats found their way inside and accidentally fell into the deep well. I could hear their cries for help late at night from my bedroom window but was helpless to save them from certain death.

Our house was built of large blocks of stone and had three bedrooms that opened onto a large central living room. Down the hallway was the TV room, dining room, kitchen, laundry room and two bathrooms. It also had five separate entrances scattered in different parts of the house. The large drafty windows and doors along with the ten-meter (33 feet) high ceilings made the house a cold and dreary place. From the time it was built, the house received minimal internal updates with the exception of the exposed electrical wiring, which my dad modernized and concealed behind the walls.

The original residence my grandfather built was a two-story house with a red brick roof. Later, my dad removed the brick roof and added three more apartments on top and three retail stores on the side, which he rented.

Before the civil war, many Israeli Jews vacationed in our village and rented apartments from my dad. In 1974, one of the Jewish tenants told my mom that they would not be returning the following year: "Your country will be destroyed by a civil war," said the Israeli woman, "so you won't see us next year."

My mom was perplexed by this information as no one suspected anything or knew of an impending war. Shortly after, all the Jews in Lebanon vanished and less than a year later, the civil war broke out.

During the winter, only our TV room was heated by an old-fashioned kerosene-burning radiator, which was vented through metal piping extending out through a hole in the ceiling. At night, the rest of the drafty house became bone-chilling cold as the hallway doors and windows swung back and forth by the infiltrating currents of cold wind and the high and low pitches of squeaks and vibrations whimpered and moaned restlessly throughout the house as we slept under piles of blankets.

The house was situated in the center of a five-acre piece of land, which was meticulously looked after to by two full time gardeners when my grandfather was alive. The land was divided into three tiers:

The Burning Cedars

An upper tier served as the entrance to the house and was planted with several kinds of flowering vegetation along with an aboveground circular cement fishpond. The middle tier was the orchard complete with plum, fig and apple trees and several varieties of grape vines. The lower tier housed the chicken coop adjacent to a spacious garden where the chickens were allowed to run free.

After my grandfather passed away, the land fell into disarray and with the exception of the upper-tiered garden, which my grandmother tended to along with the fruit trees, the remaining acres were un-kept and overgrown with weeds.

RAMZY BAROODY

Our house in the village of Aley shortly after it was built by my grandfather in 1926.

The house seventy years later in 1996, badly damaged by the war.

The Burning Cedars

The teacher brought me home from school one afternoon for, as she put it, "slightly twisting my finger after falling down." My arm was swollen to twice its size and my mom immediately knew that it was broken. I spent a month at home with a cast on my arm recuperating. I'm holding a flag with its hollow handle filled with sweet mints, standing across the street from my house in the background.

RAMZY BAROODY

My uncle loved trains. He took me to the station every afternoon to watch as the train departed into the tunnel on its way up the mountain to villages in the north.

The Burning Cedars

CHAPTER THREE

CHRISTMAS

At the start of the civil war, the fighting was limited to parts of the capital Beirut between the Lebanese Army and the Palestinian refugees. In their camps in what is to be known "West Beirut," the Palestinian refugees had organized a well-equipped army that they frequently and proudly displayed throughout the streets of Beirut. Their camps became well-fortified bunkers with miles of underground tunnels used to transport army men and ammunition.

It did not take long for the Lebanese Christian and Muslim civilians to form their own opposing armed militias and the fighting turned into a religious rather than an ethnic one. With the army split along religions affiliations, the country fell into a bloody and vicious civil war that everyone knew was to be a long one.

Before the war, I enjoyed a happy childhood although I had difficulty making friends and was uncomfortable around strangers. My friends were my cousins whom I saw quite frequently, especially those on my mother's side, as they lived in the same village as I.

I was also close to my cousins on my fathers' side, who vacationed in our village during the summer and wintered in Beirut. Aunt Grace, my fathers' sister, had four children, two of whom are close to my age.

The Burning Cedars

She married a prominent dentist and the family was very comfortable financially.

Her Beirut apartment was cheerful and inviting always smelling of freshly cut flowers and baked cookies although it always felt oppressively hot compared to my old and drafty mountain house.

Every Christmas aunt Grace would put up two Christmas trees, full of decorations with lots of presents underneath. My dad's brother, uncle Tony dressed up as Santa and handed out gifts to their lucky recipients.

He would call out our names in his deep "Santa voice," as he handed out presents followed by a gentle slap on our behinds with a wooden spoon he held in his hand. I never understood nor questioned the significance of his wooden spoon or how it became a part of his Santa costume.

On Christmas Eve in 1973, my cousins and I huddled together on the floor of their apartment eagerly waiting for our names to be called. The six-foot tall red and white Santa emerged from behind the curtain complete with his wooden spoon in hand.

One by one he handed out presents from his red Santa bag until at the end I realized that there were none left. Sadly I watched as my cousins joyfully opened their many presents while I cowered in the corner disappointed and hurt. I tried very hard to hold back the tears but the look of grief and disbelief was clearly evident on my face.

I felt someone take my hand and lead me toward the front door.

RAMZY BAROODY

My older cousin Rhona had asked her father for $100 liras and we rode down the elevator to the toy store on the ground floor of their apartment building, where she said to me: "Pick out anything you want."

Earlier that evening, one of my cousins had been gifted a radio in the shape of the Goofy character from Disney. I wanted a similar radio so I picked out the Pinocchio- shaped radio which cost exactly $100 liras, grabbed Rhona's hand and ran toward the elevator.

I couldn't wait to show my parents what I had gotten for Christmas, and when we got back to the third floor apartment, I saw them arguing in the corner about neglecting to buy me a present.

Even though my father was very prudent with his money, he was a kind and loving man whose frugality and unremitting concern with money permeated every facet of his life, including his relationship with his family. "I thought his aunt Grace was buying him presents since we were invited to her house" illogically argued my dad.

As I walked in the door, my mom ran over and took me in her arms, and with tears in her eyes whispered: "I'm so sorry we didn't buy you any presents."

"Look" I said proudly "I bought myself a Pinocchio radio!"

This radio I treasure to this day and it still works.

The Burning Cedars

Uncle Tony dressed as Santa, wooden spoon in hand at aunt Grace's house in Beirut. With a big smile on my face, I am holding my wrapped "last minute" present, a Pinocchio-shaped Radio.

My Pinocchio radio survived the war and countless moves intact and it still works!

RAMZY BAROODY

The Burning Cedars

CHAPTER FOUR

NOT FOR SALE

My grandfather, Shucry Baroody, my dads' father, was a prominent and respected physician in our town during the early 1900s. He made a very good living and was able to build several residences around town, one of which we lived in until it was sold in 1979. At the start of the civil war, my dad refused to sell the building even though our lives were in great danger by the constant bombardment from Beirut. We were one of the very few Christian families remaining in this predominantly Druze village, knowing that many Christian families had been massacred by the Druze militias. For months the bombs fell within a few yards from our house while we huddled in terror inside.

Across the street from our house was the town city hall, a prime target for shelling during the war as it was converted to a militia outpost. Even so my dad remained adamant against selling and moving away. Several shells hit the top floors of our five-story building, and fortunately none of the tenants were staying there at the time. In the mornings the shelling would usually subside giving us enough time to scour the neighborhood looking for open stores to buy food and bread.

I would walk through our backyard collecting large pieces of shrapnel and bullet casings that had fallen there on the previous night. Such items were a novelty at the beginning of the war and as a kid, I was fascinated by such malevolent tools of killing and destruction. Before long, I had a bag-full of twisted pieces of metal and various bullet sizes that I eventually decided to throw away as the war dragged on. Eventually, such items littered the streets and backyards and one had to be careful when walking around as the jagged edges of shrapnels of various sizes and shapes could cause serious lacerations to ones legs or hands if touched. It was not long before I experienced first hand the damage these metal pieces could do when they penetrate the human body and the pain and suffering they can inflict.

The Burning Cedars

CHAPTER FIVE

LODY

Even though my dad came from a prominent and affluent family, my mom did not. She and her four siblings lived in a dilapidated one-bedroom house with their mother, grandmother Souad. Their father, grandpa Joseph, was rarely around and no one really knew his whereabouts or what he did for a living. All we knew was that he worked as a taxi driver for some time and little else. He would disappear for months then show up suddenly to, as he would put it "check up on the kids."

Many years later we discovered that he had another wife and children in Beirut and was likely living with them most of the time. I have faint memories of grandpa Joseph and the only time I saw him was when he came to our house asking for a handout from my mom. He was known for his extreme generosity and often gave the clothes on his back to strangers and vagrants while he went cold, hungry and penniless.

Grandmother Souad was a kind and loving person with a small frail posture. She managed to raise four children with almost no means of support. She depended on financial assistance from family members, particularly her husbands' brother, who was well off and

The Burning Cedars

worked as the manager of the largest and most famous hotel in Lebanon at that time, Hotel Tanius in Aley.

Being the oldest of her siblings, my mother Lody tried to take on the responsibility of caring for and supporting the family.
At the age of seventeen, she dropped out of school and worked as a telephone operator at the local phone company.

The high school nuns of the *Two Sacred Hearts* where my mother attended used to come to the house inquiring for the whereabouts of my mother. The *Two Sacred Hearts* was a private Catholic school, and the nuns refused to admit students unable to pay their tuition.

My grandmother begged the nuns to keep my mother in school even though she could not afford the payments and sometimes, they would reluctantly agree.

In return for their "generosity," the nuns would make an announcement to the entire class that my mother, along with several other students had not paid the tuition and were freeloaders, to the laughs and mocks of their classmates.

At seventeen, my mother became the breadwinner in the family. With her first paycheck, she purchased new living room furniture for the house. My mother also loved fashion and with her tall and stylish figure, she carried herself with an elegance of a wealthy socialite.

On many occasion, affluent summer vacationers took interest in my mother as she strolled along the boulevard in her new dress and slightly aloof demeanor. She could hear them inquiring "who is she?" and "where does she live?"

Many tried to approach her and followed her home only to be dismayed by her living conditions and economic and social status.

My mom had beautiful brown eyes, and was approached on several occasions by photographers wanting to take pictures of her eyes to be used as store displays for eyeglasses, but she declined.

Aside from her outward physical beauty, my mother had the benefit of a strong moral fiber along with a fundamental and unconditional love and support for everyone in her life especially her family. She raised us with the same values and principles and taught us to respect all people no matter their religion, race or nationality and to not judge anyone based on outward appearances.

The Burning Cedars

Her looks earned her the nickname "The Lebanese Sophia Loren" but it was her big brown eyes that caught the attention of many photographers wanting to capture their beauty in store display ads.

She declined.

RAMZY BAROODY

Strolling down the main street of Aley with her friends in the afternoon, my mother (center) turned heads.

The Burning Cedars

CHAPTER SIX

COURTSHIP

    *O*ne summer day walking with her friends around town, my mother caught the eye of a very tall and handsome young man from a well to do family in town. His name was Tony Baroody. In those days, a man expressed his interest in a woman by following her around town hoping to catch a brief stare or a smile. If he senses interest, he would eventually exchange words.

    Several months went by but Tony would not approach or speak to my mother. Shortly after, another young man began to pursue my mother relentlessly. Through several inquiries my mom found out that this man was Tony's' older brother, Bahjat.

    My mother, a tall and elegant woman, turned many heads as she strolled down the main street with her friends heading to the movies every afternoon. Bahjat continued to pursue her daily and everywhere she went. "He's following you again," her friends whispered. A shy and timid person by nature, my mother kept her head down and walked faster to avoid eye contact with Bahjat.

    Initially, my dad did not appeal to my mother and she even disliked him for being unrelenting in his pursuit. For seven years, my dad pursued my mother and turned up everywhere she went but my

The Burning Cedars

mom continued to give him the cold shoulder. My mom recalls an incident of when my dad finally decided to "break the ice" between them seven years into the chase: "Bahjat decided to give me a present. I was standing in the garden of our house and your father walked by and threw a small box into the grass under my feet and continued on his way without saying a word. I opened the box expecting a ring or jewelry. Instead there was a single cookie inside. Everyone had warned me, including his closest friends, that he was odd and stingy and this confirmed it."

My mom continued, "I must've been blind or stupid allowing this man to even come close to me, but I guess fate stepped in and here we are."

Sometimes in life, personal circumstances can blind us to the truth and compel us to make unwise decisions to our detriment. My mom's life of poverty and privation overshadowed the numerous shortcomings she saw in my dad. Nevertheless, she did agree to marry him and it was far from a fairytale wedding!

RAMZY BAROODY

*My dad relentlessly chased after my mother,
even when her mother warned her against speaking
or even looking at him.*

The Burning Cedars

CHAPTER SEVEN

WEDDING RING

After my grandfather passed away, my dad controlled all the household finances. Neither his younger brother Tony nor Sister Grace had the desire or aptitude to manage the family estate.

My dad experimented with several careers before settling into the import/export clothing business. After graduating from college, he opened a grocery store selling sandwiches, groceries and liquor. When clients came in wanting a sandwich, he would tell them to make it themselves. They would gladly jump behind the counter stacking cold cuts three-feet high on a slice of bread. Six months later, the store went under.

Uncle Tony was a journalist for the prominent entertainment paper *Al-Shabaka* or *The Net*, reporting on news from the entertainment, radio, and TV industry.

My grandmother Zafer stayed at home bossing the maids and the gardeners. Grandma Zafer was a tall thin energetic and harsh woman. She had married my grandfather Shucry in 1931 at the age of 28, he was 58! He was also her cousin.

Unlike Grandma Zafer, my grandfather was a kind, easygoing, and caring man who frequently battled the snow and ice late into the

The Burning Cedars

night to attend to his sick patients, many of who were poor and unable to afford a payment, but he would treat them regardless for free.

My grandfather was a respected doctor in the village and was loved by everyone. Later in his career he opened his own pharmacy and named it *Baroody Pharmacy, which* survives to this day under the same name and open for business.

In November 1956, my mom and dad eloped. She was 21, he was 23. The wedding consisted of a short ceremony in the towns' protestant church with two of my dads' friends as witnesses.

At the conclusion of the ceremony, the priest asked for the exchange of the weddings rings. My dad had conveniently forgotten to purchase them. He turned to his friend and asked if he could borrow his ring to finalize the ceremony.

Embarrassed, his friend acquiesced taking off his own wedding ring and handing it to my dad. He then turned and whispered to my mother: "make sure your husband gives me back my ring after the ceremony."

RAMZY BAROODY

*In 1931, My Grandfather, Dr. Shucry Baroody
married his cousin, Zafer Baroody, who
was thirty years his junior.*

The Burning Cedars

*My dad was more concerned with balancing the books
than helping customers.
After six months, his store went under.*

RAMZY BAROODY

The Burning Cedars

CHAPTER EIGHT

ZAFER

*F*ollowing the short wedding ceremony, my parents headed home. My mom was unaware that she would be living with my grandmother and my uncle. My dad had no intention of forfeiting the income from one of his rental apartments.

My mother also found out that my grandmother had no knowledge of this wedding and took an immediate dislike to the new bride. As the newlyweds walked up the garden path, my grandmother was on the front porch knitting.

"Good afternoon mother-in-law" my mom said with a smile. My grandmother did not reply, turned to my dad saying "You have lowered your standing in the community by marrying this trash," gathered her knitting yarn and walked inside. My mom was in utter shock and cried hysterically that entire day. My dad's comforting words to her were "don't pay my mother any attention."

Early the following morning, my mom was shaken out of bed by my grandmother: "We're not running a hotel here. Get up and start cleaning the house top to bottom."

This was the first time in her life this naive and immature 21 year-old bride had to confront a much older, headstrong, privileged, cruel, and controlling mother-in-law and was at a loss for what to do. The only path she knew to take was that of total submission and to acquiesce to every command given. My grandmother played this scenario to her full advantage by mistreating my mother verbally and mentally the entire time they lived together. She treated my mother as the housemaid and my mother went along with it.

Domineering and ruthless, my grandmother lived her life in a manner which afforded her the greatest gain and benefit from everyone around her, with total disregard to any harm or negative consequence this may inflict on others.

She only liked and related to those who held similar values and ideals as her and mistreated everyone else. Although she was not anti-Semitic in any way, my grandmother was an outspoken supporter of the German chancellor Adolph Hitler. She liked his ruthless style of leadership and control, and after the Second World War, she declared that Hitler's death was a loss to humanity as he was a great leader.
Even my grandmothers' sister once referred to her as a "me, myself and I kind of person."

In comparison, my mother was the embodiment of kindness and generosity and a "what can I do for you" kind of person, always placing the comfort and happiness of others above of her own. It was thus inevitable for these two personalities to collide, transforming each others' lives into living hell and a miserable kind of existence.

The Burning Cedars

*The new bride one day after her wedding.
With a gleam in her eye and a smile
on her face, she was unaware
of what awaited her inside.*

RAMZY BAROODY

*During an evening stroll, my grandmother
clearly unhappy with her company!
My dad with a look of sadness,
was always caught in the middle.*

The Burning Cedars

CHAPTER NINE

THE FISH POND

On September 17, 1958, my mother gave birth to my brother, whom they named Shucry after my grandfather. My brother was a mischievous child always getting into trouble. At the age of five, he decided to take a walk into town by himself. My mother got hysterical trying to find him to no avail. Half an hour later, he was returned home by a neighbor who saw him walking down the main street by himself and recognized him. My mom frantically ran outside to collect him, and noticed that my grandmother had been sitting on the front porch all that time, calmly rocking back and forth in her chair knitting. "Didn't you see Shucry walk past you out the gate and down the street, why didn't you stop him?" my mother asked. "He'll be fine," my indifferent and cold grandmother muttered in her usual deep and curt tone of voice.

My uncle recalls a similar incident that happened to him when he was my brothers' age. He was playing around the fishpond in the front yard when he slipped and fell in. As he was close to drowning, he yelled for his mother, who was sitting nearby for help. She refused to get up and help him. "He needs to be taught a lesson not to play around the pond" she told the maid, who then rushed to my uncle's aid

The Burning Cedars

and pulled him out. My uncle never forgave his mother for not saving him from almost drowning on that day.

Many years later when I was six, I also fell into the same pond and was close to drowning. I vividly remember falling backwards into the pond and looking up as I sank towards the bottom and seeing the large goldfish as they swam past me with their dazzling red and white scales reflecting the sunlight entering the water. It was a surreal experience, which happened so quickly that I did not have time to panic. Luckily, my cousin Rhona was nearby and pulled me out to safety within seconds. A few days later, my dad removed the pond and filled the hole with cement.

My cousin Roula and I playing by the fishpond, which was kept half full after I fell in until my dad removed it completely.

My mother with my older brother, Shucry, whom despite his unruly behavior as a child, managed to avoid falling into the fishpond.

The Burning Cedars

CHAPTER TEN

DEPRESSION

My mother did not plan on having another child after my brother was born. She had a miserable home life with a cruel and domineering mother-in-law and an unsupportive husband, who buried himself in his work preferring to steer clear of intervening on my mothers' behalf against his own mother.

Nevertheless, when my brother was six, my mother became pregnant with me. On November 16, 1964, I was born in a Beirut hospital. A few days later, my mother brought me home and had not yet decided what to name me. Ten days later, on November 26, my dad headed to the newborn records office to register my birth under the name my mother had chosen, Oscar. On his way there, he ran into one of his relatives by the name of Ramzy. He returned home an hour later with my birth certificate and the name Ramzy Baroody, birth date November 26, 1964.

After I was born, my mother suffered a postpartum depression that left her totally incapable to raise a baby. She was unable to perform the simplest of tasks like changing diapers or preparing feeding bottles. My dad in his usual "caring and supporting" manner, did not want to be bothered and moved out of the bedroom and into his

mothers'. My mom begged him to prepare the feeding bottles and change my diapers but he wanted nothing to do with it. "There's nothing wrong with you, it's your job to take care of the baby" was his cold reply.

Luckily, Uncle Tony stepped in and gave my mom the support she so badly needed. He took charge of the midnight feedings and the changing of the diapers as my dad slept soundly in the next room. My mother visited several doctors to treat her depression but the medication was making her worse. For the months that followed, she slept and cried constantly with no improvement.

Finally she visited a doctor who prescribed a new and experimental medication, which gradually improved her condition.

My mothers' total reliance on my uncle formed an unexpected and special bond between him and myself. Being a childless bachelor, he looked at me as his son and treated me as such for the rest of his life.

RAMZY BAROODY

My uncle looked after and accompanied us everywhere we went during my mothers' depression while my father was at work.

The Burning Cedars

CHAPTER ELEVEN

UNCLE TONY

Uncle Tony was a loving and caring man who spoiled me with his kindness, generosity, and affection. I adored him and was constantly by his side wherever he went. He walked me to school every morning and waited for me at the end of the day. He never refused me anything and I was always number one in his life, as he was in mine.

My uncles' unwavering attention and love for me did not go unnoticed by my brother Shucry, who received little of it. His jealousy boiled over into loud and sometimes physical confrontations with my uncle. My brother gradually distanced himself from me and our relationship has remained subdued ever since.

Although I love my brother, we are two very different people in every way. Shucry was a mischievous kid who grew up to be a mellow and religiously conservative person. With me he was distant, indifferent and un-engaging. Furthermore, I was the comedian in the family and loved to make people laugh.

Always with a smile on my face and a quick wit, in familiar surroundings I was funny, engaging and well liked. This annoyed my brother, as I would constantly detract attention from him everywhere

The Burning Cedars

we went. Little did he know that I've used my humor to hide the uneasiness I felt around strangers in social settings.

Making others laugh is the best way to break the ice and to get people to like you. Not only did I want to be liked, but I also felt a certain degree of satisfaction and solace in doing so. All the attention and special treatment I received from everyone angered my brother even more and he ostracized me for it. This steered us even further apart straining an already volatile relationship.

Yet with my uncle constantly by my side, he filled the many voids in my life; the lack of friends, the indifferent and distant brother, the workaholic and miserly father and the depressed and weak mother. And for my uncle, a childless bachelor, I fulfilled his need of caring for and loving a child of his own.

RAMZY BAROODY

Uncle Tony and I were inseparable. I was the son he never had and he was the kind, generous, loving uncle I adored.

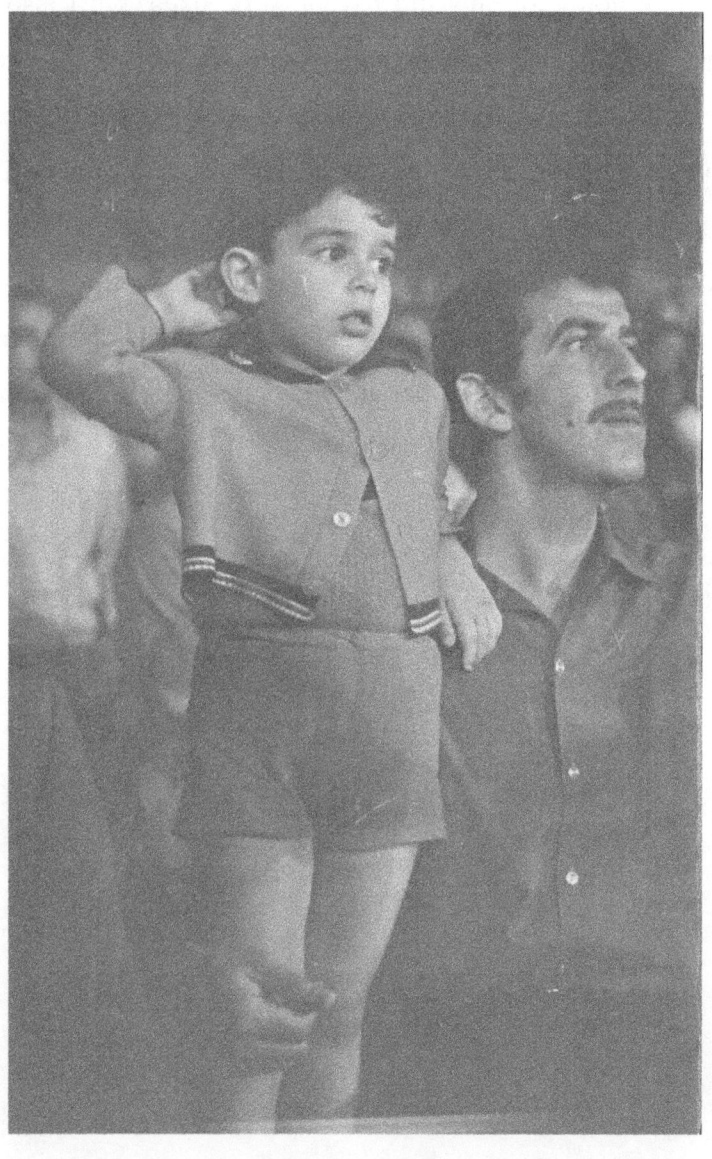

Uncle Tony and I at the circus.

The Burning Cedars

Walking back home after purchasing corn on the cob from the old woman who sold them by the side of the road across from the train station in Aley during the summer.

RAMZY BAROODY

The Burning Cedars

CHAPTER TWELVE

BEIRUT EVANGELICAL

*M*y dad always wanted us to get the best education money could buy, so he enrolled my brother and I in a prestigious elementary school in the southern outskirts of Beirut in the town of Haddas called the *Beirut Evangelical School* which was founded by a Christian British missionary.

Although the school was quite a distance from our home in the mountains, it was the best English school in the country with a great reputation. The superintendent and founder, Mr. White, was a gray-haired, middle-aged stern British man with piercing blue eyes. He walked up and down the school hallways during the day peaking into each classroom through a window in the door. Seeing him in the doorway sent shivers down our spines while we sat frozen in our seats.

I have always had difficulty socializing and making friends, and although I felt awkward and lonely in school, I was a good student academically and never got into trouble.

I was an un-athletic and overweight kid who did not enjoy sports or after school activities.

I dreaded the hour-long noon lunch break, as I had no friends to play with and anxiously awaited the bell to ring signaling us to return to class. During our lunch hour, I disappeared and hid in the olive groves across the street from the school. That place was my sanctuary where I felt comfortable and isolated, as I sat there patiently waiting to hear the school bell.

On rainy days we had to play indoors in the school hallways and I used to spend the time walking back and forth each floor of the four-story building pretending to be looking for someone. I would sometimes look for my brother but, as usual, he was nowhere to be found.

In all the years we went to school together, my brother never made an attempt to look for his younger brother nor inquire for my whereabouts or if I needed anything. After we got dropped off in the morning, I would not see him again until we got picked up at the end of the day. Several times during the school day I would walk past his classroom to see him sitting at his desk, which made me both angry and relieved at the same time.

Growing up I was never given an allowance. My dad always told me that if I needed money, I should ask him for it but when I did, he never had it. My mom packed me a sandwich daily to take to school, which I usually ate during our ten o'clock break. By lunchtime I would be starving as I watched the kids line up to buy their lunches from the concession stands.

The smell of my favorite food, oregano pie, filled the air and was too much to take, so I retreated to my sanctuary in the woods.

The Burning Cedars

Several times I saw my brother at the stand purchasing food but in his usual manner, he ignored me as he ran past to disappear into the crowd. At the end of each school year, the school published its yearbook with pictures, articles and news about events, student activities and faculty interviews. We anxiously lined up during the last day of school to receive our yearbooks and tore through it looking for our pictures and, for those who had friends, for their pictures as well. Needless to say, with one exception in 1972 when our class picture was published along with our class teacher, Miss Kai, my picture never appeared in the yearbook, as I never got involved in any after-school activities.

In June of 1974, our principal, Mr. White, planned a very special end of school year event. In the garden behind our church, he organized a dedication ceremony with all the students and faculty in attendance. Photographers snapped pictures as he planted a small Lebanese cedar trees, then placed a special plaque in the ground commemorating this occasion. In his short speech, he expressed his fondness for the Lebanese cedar, which symbolizes longevity and endurance, and wished the same for his beloved school and for the country.

Although the Lebanese cedar takes thousands of years to grow and mature, the planting of the cedar was a beautiful gesture, even if symbolic, of this British man's fondness and appreciation for my country and all it has to offer, and we all enjoyed that special final day immensely.

RAMZY BAROODY

*The first time my picture (second row from back on far left)
appeared in the school yearbook at Beirut Evangelical
with our class teacher, Ms. Kai in 1972.
It was an awkward and lonely time for
me as I had difficulty making friends.*

The Burning Cedars

Beirut Evangelical School For Boys founder and Principal, Mr. White. His stern demeanor and piercing blue eyes stirred fear and obedience in all of us.

I held on dearly to the 1972-1973 school yearbook where my picture, as part of a class portrait was published.

RAMZY BAROODY

The Burning Cedars

CHAPTER THIRTEEN

THE PUNISHMENT

*E*very December, our school organized a beautiful Christmas show by decorating the adjoining church with beautiful ornaments full of vibrant colors of gold, red and yellow. I was recruited for the school performance two years in a row playing an angel announcing the birth of Christ and one of the kings who brought presents to welcome baby Jesus. My parents, however, never got to see me on stage as they were habitually late both years, arriving an hour after the show had started.

It is perhaps a Lebanese custom to be habitually late and to have little regard for deadlines or promptness. To this day, I struggle to keep time or to be punctual for any function and am habitually late. Rarely did my brother or I arrive to school on time in the morning, which infuriated our teachers and landed us in detention.

In 1971, both my dad and mom had had enough of the constant bickering between my mother and grandmother. For once my mother took a stand and insisted that we get our own place, so my dad rented a spacious apartment in the *Hamra* district of Beirut, an upscale and trendy part of the city which was close to my dads' work and our school. The school bus stop was literally across the street from our building yet being habitually late, we were never on time to catch it. Some days my brother and I were able to run across town to catch the bus six blocks away but on most days, my dad had to drive us or we would have to take a taxi to school.

Our Beirut adventure lasted exactly one year and back to Aley we went. My dad complained daily that he had to pay rent, or as he put it "throw his money away" needlessly when we could be living in our old house for free. My brother also complained that he missed the outdoor space and his chickens and pigeons.

My mother and I loved living in Beirut but we had little say in the matter and the final decision to go back home was made by my dad at the end of that year. So we packed and headed back to Aley where, without delay, the daily arguing and bickering resumed again. Furthermore, as it turned out, living close to school had little effect on our morning arrival times to the constant complaints of our teachers.

The punishment for tardiness was ten spanks with a wooden ruler on the palm of the hand. Luckily however, I was exempt from such punishment due to my dads' intervention on my behalf.

It was after our midterm examinations when our class teacher announced that some students who had arrived late at the day of the exam had performed very poorly and would be punished the following day. The punishment for a low or failing grade ranged from ten to twenty spanks with the ruler in addition to the extra ten spanks for tardiness.

The Burning Cedars

The next morning on our way to school, I told my dad of what was possibly awaiting me at school once I got there but he said nothing.

We pulled into the school's parking lot and instead of pulling up to the side to drop us off, he calmly parked the car and shut off the engine, still saying nothing. We got out and my dad took my hand and walked me into the principals' office where all the teachers were gathered for their morning briefing before classes began.

By then he was clearly steaming from both ears and stood in the middle of the office while all eyes were on us: "I do not approve of anyone touching my son or punishing him for any reason" he announced furiously. "If I hear of anyone hitting my son, I will pull him out of the school and there will be hell to pay, do I make myself clear?" The teachers and principal sat there dumbfounded as this man read them the riot act, after which they assured him that his wishes will be fully respected.

Parents raise their children the way they were themselves raised. My dad was a very permissive father and never laid a hand on us nor punished us for any reason.

The only time he yelled was during his afternoon naps when we disturbed him with any noise. "RAMZY" he yelled and that was enough to quiet us down.

My mother, on the other hand, knew of only one form of punishment. She would take off one of her shoes and hurl it at us from across the room, rarely striking us.

One time I got so mad after the shoe went flying across the room that I picked it up and threw it out the balcony into the backyard. My mother was furious and decided that a follow-up act was in order with the other shoe, which was also picked up and tossed into the garden. She chased me around the house barefoot until I ran into the yard making faces at her. Standing in the doorway, she screamed and promised reprisals upon my return.

As usual, my grandmother intervened on my behalf, and the retaliation was never executed: "In this house we do not hit children" my grandmother ordered as I took cover behind her making faces and sticking my tongue out at my mother.

I am certain that my grandmother's motive behind her intervening on my behalf was less out of concern and more about her deep hatred for my mother. My grandmother wanted any excuse to admonish my mother at every turn. Regardless, at the time it served my needs and I was grateful for it.

The Burning Cedars

My grandmother despised my mother yet she was kind and loving towards me. She often protected me from my mothers' "flying shoe" most likely to assert her dominance and because she knew this will upset and contradict my mother.

RAMZY BAROODY

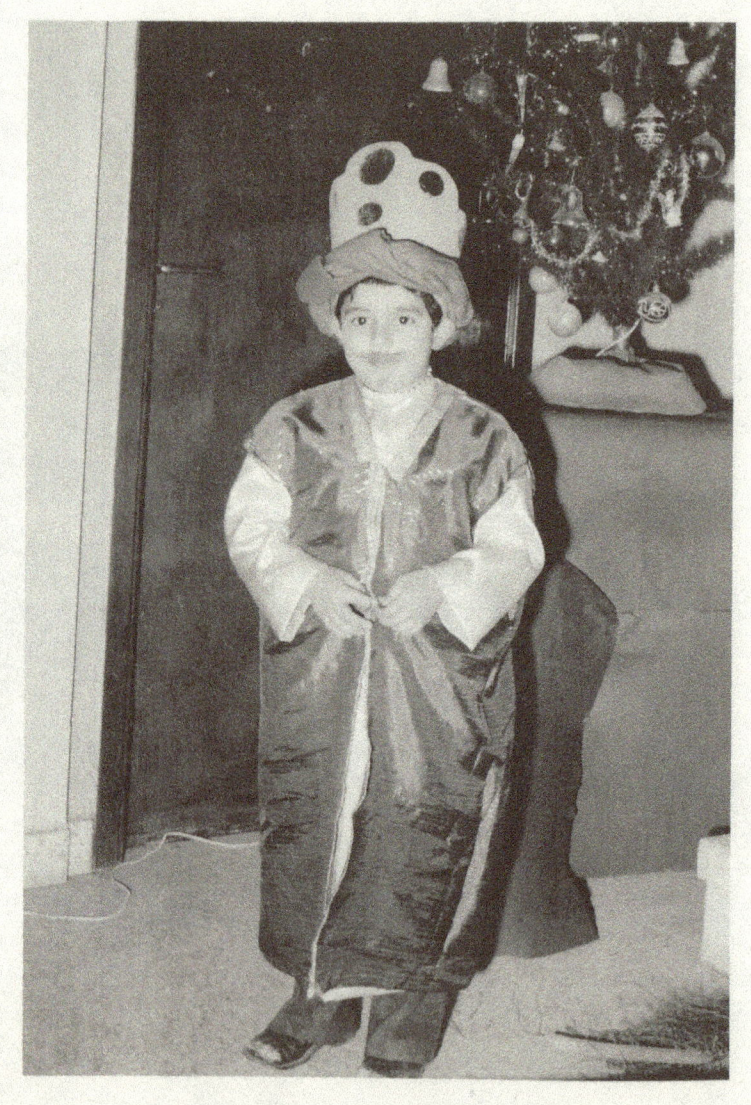

I portrayed a king announcing the birth of Christ in our school's Christmas show. Unfortunately, my parents arrived late and missed my performance, which upset me terribly.

The Burning Cedars

CHAPTER FOURTEEN

DISPLAY OF AFFECTION

Although my grandmother despised my mother, she never showed any animosity or hatred towards me. In her limited capacity to love or show affection, I believe that she did love me. She also recognized how much I loved and was loved by my uncle, which endeared me to her even more. Her pet name for me was *Mannix* from the TV show by the same name. I don't know why she associated me with an American private eye detective, perhaps she liked that name or the actor, Mike Connors. Another nickname she called me was "daabool." A literal translation would be "the round object" referring to my rotund figure, but "butterball" also applies yet not any more flattering.

Grandmother had difficulty displaying positive emotions, as she probably thought it projected weakness of character. I've been told by both my uncle and father that they do not recall ever being kissed or hugged by my grandmother. When I was a kid, if someone tried to kiss or hug me, my grandmother jumped up yelling: "he doesn't like to be kissed or touched," which was farthest from the truth, but I went along with it.

The Burning Cedars

With the exception of my uncle and my mother, both my dad and brother were also limited in their displays of any physical affection towards me. One particular incident in 1973 still upsets me to this day.

On a beautiful Saturday afternoon, my family and I were strolling back from a trip to the hills surrounding our home. As we got ready to cross the street, I reached over and grabbed my brother's hand when he abruptly pulled away and scolded me for doing so, telling me that this kind of behavior is inappropriate. This kind of upbringing has a profound affect on a child and to this day I endeavor with great difficulty to display affection towards any family member. I rarely hug or kiss my mother and when she questions it, my answer is always "You know that I love you, why do I need to show it?"

RAMZY BAROODY

The Burning Cedars

CHAPTER FIFTEEN

REVELATION

On a cold night in January, uncle Tony experienced a life-altering encounter, which haunted him for the rest of his life, and left a deep emotional scar both on him and the family.

As everyone slept, a loud scream was heard from my uncle's room, best described as a blood-curdling wail or screech. Everyone rushed in and saw my uncle sitting up in bed, white as a ghost and tongue-tied. He did not even look like himself, his facial features somehow looked different as he sobbed loudly and uncontrollably, unable to speak. An hour went by when my uncle was able to speak a few words but with great difficulty and a pronounced stutter: "Jesus appeared to me" he kept saying over and over as tears flowed from his eyes, "he was standing there" pointing to the corner of the room, "his light was very bright and pure white almost blinding me as he approached my bed, then he stopped at the foot of the bed and said to me 'Tony, why have you forsaken me?' he said it twice then disappeared." The family was in shock and did not know what to do. My father ran over to the family priest at three am who immediately came over and commenced to pray and read from the Bible alongside a whimpering tongue-tied Tony. The following morning, the family witnessed something they were not prepared to see. My uncle's face looked as if it were sun burnt, and peeling. He was barely able to see and still unable to speak.

At first the family thought that Tony had been dreaming, but the physical implications on his face proved otherwise.

My uncle never elaborated on what "Jesus" meant by asking him such a question and perhaps, none of us wanted to know.

It took several weeks for uncle Tony to physically recover from his encounter, yet for the rest of his life never fully recovered mentally or emotionally. He struggled with a debilitating nervous breakdown, which was compounded by the many circumstances most people have to endure in life. Yet unlike healthy people who can deal with life struggles and bypass difficulties, uncle Tony could not, and the slightest set back could send him into an abyss of deep depression and confusion. He was like a helpless child trapped in a man's body, unable to cope with simple tasks, which we all take for granted as a part of normal living.

This was compounded by the extra-ordinary pressures of war and family separation and reached its tragic climax many years later with the passing of his mother and sister within one year of each other, leaving him alone, depressed and suicidal.

The Burning Cedars

*My uncle was never the same after the night Jesus
appeared to him.
He fell into a deep depression from which he never recovered.*

… → "FIFA"

The Burning Cedars

CHAPTER SIXTEEN

LITHIUM

As children, we pick up on subtle clues from our surroundings, many of which we're unable to process or fully understand till later in life, if at all. Around the age of twelve, I began to realize that there was something mentally unstable with my uncle. He suffered from a severe form of depression and was self-medicating through correspondence with a doctor in England whom he read about in the papers. Monthly shipments arrived to our house from England containing boxes of a new and controversial anti-depressant drug called Lithium. Prior, my uncle experimented with numerous self-prescribed medications, but none helped him as much as Lithium.

In Lebanon, you did not need a doctor's prescription to buy drugs from the pharmacy, and my uncle took full advantage of this. Lithium side effects included tiredness, dry mouth and cold sores, and my uncle exhibited all three, otherwise, his mental state seemed to be improved while on this drug.

He would come home from work daily around noon and fall asleep in his favorite chair in the TV room till dinnertime. Get back up, eat dinner then go back to bed till the following morning. Uncle Tony was an early riser and felt his best mentally early in the morning. He had a habit of singing and whistling loudly in the kitchen as he prepared his morning coffee. His singing and whistling echoed vociferously throughout the house waking everyone up at the crack of dawn. We were all glad that he was feeling better that none of us complained about his raucous early morning whistling and singing.

My uncle idolized a famous Egyptian singer named *Abdul Wahab*. To him, there were no other singers or composers, and all the rest were just imitators and wannabees. To his delight, uncle Tony had the good fortune of meeting Abdul Wahab several times, and he wrote about him weekly in his newspaper column.

We always made fun of my uncles' undying devotion to this singer and teased him endlessly about changing the title of his newspaper page to "How I love Abdul-Wahab!"

Furthermore, my uncle firmly believed that he sounded like Abdul-Wahab, and that he could flawlessly sing his songs. Using his influence as a journalist, he convinced the *Voice Of The Middle East* radio station manager to allow him to give a live rendition of his favorite Abdul-Wahab song. After uncle Tony's live radio performance, his odd Uncle, Samuel, expressed to him in a way only he could or would, what he thought of his singing: "So you mean to tell me you sang and left the station and no one beat you up for it?" Unfortunately for my Uncle, Samuel was known to be an eccentric and strange person who spoke his mind without regard to anyone's feelings. A trait that seems to run in the Baroody family.

The Burning Cedars

Uncle Tony (standing) with his idol, Egyptian singer/songwriter Abdul-Wahab at a recording session in Beirut.

RAMZY BAROODY

The Burning Cedars

CHAPTER SEVENTEEN

SABAH

I admired and envied Uncle Tony meeting and interviewing celebrities for his weekly column. Of particular interest to me were a famous female singer and performer who went by the name of Sabah. Back then, two female singers dominated the music arena in Lebanon: Sabah and Fairouz.

Fairouz was more down to earth than glamorous both in her stage presence and fashion style. She relied more on her impeccable singing ability and a remarkable voice, which earned her the title "the woman with the angelic voice." She was also fortunate in having an equally talented songwriter and manager for a husband.

In contrast, Sabah was an over-the-top, high-spirited singer and actress who projected life, passion and excitement. Aside from singing and showmanship, Sabah had two major weak spots in her life: fashion and men. She spent all of her earnings on dresses and had been married nine times to men who were at times thirty years her junior.

She wore over-flowing dresses and huge blond wigs and was always seen with a smile on her face.

She declared during many of her interviews that she lived a carefree life and does not allow negativity to enter her life. As she got older it became evident that her life was far from a fairytale and she in fact sustained a sad and tragic existence.

When I was thirteen, uncle Tony arranged a very special surprise for me, knowing how much I loved and adored Sabah. He was to interview her at her home and wanted me to come along. I was overjoyed and extremely nervous.

On our way to her summer home in the outskirts of Aley called *ras-al-jabal* or *top of the mountain*, I was sweating uncontrollably all over. We arrived at her apartment and by the time my uncle rang the doorbell, I was drenched in sweat and my hands visibly shaking. I turned to my uncle and he was as calm as can be. I thought to myself "What do you know, Lithium *really* works!"

As the door opened, I jumped and hid behind my uncle. After exchanging hellos my uncle turned around and said, "Oh, this is my nephew Ramzy and he's one of your biggest fans." Sabah looked around perplexed, as she could not see anyone else. Unexpectedly, my uncle took one step to the right and there I stood, shaking all over in a puddle of sweat. I looked up at her and mumbled something like "h-e-l-l-o." She then reached over to shake my hand but I just stood there stiff as a board.

My first impression of Sabah was of surprise and amazement. Although welcoming and beautiful, seeing her in a "normal" setting with her thin blond hair tied into a pony tail, without her stage wigs, her flowing dresses and tons of makeup and a plain house dress took me back slightly.

The Burning Cedars

We sat down in her living room that overlooked Beirut and the Mediterranean Sea, with its turquoise blue water glistening in the abundant sunshine. As my uncle prepared for the interview, Sabah turned to me and asked "Would you like anything to drink sweetheart?" I smiled and mumbled "Oh no thank you." What I really wanted is to stop sweating. Furthermore, it was late afternoon and the sun filled her living room making it warm and toasty, exasperating my "wettness."

Sabah then went into the kitchen and came out with a glass of ice and a bottle of 7-UP. She poured the 7-UP into the glass and told me to help myself. As much as I wanted something cold to drink, I kept imagining the glass flying out of my sweaty quivering hands and spilling all over her white carpeting. So I decided not to touch anything and I just sat there stiff and awkward. When the interview was over, Sabah said that she will be right back and a few minutes later, returned with two autographed pictures of herself and handed them to me. "These are for you sweetheart," she said with her trademark smile on her face. I reached over and took the pictures, shook her hand and walked out dazed with joy. When we got to the car I quickly looked over the pictures and began hopping up and down in my seat. My uncle was equally overjoyed for me and cautioned me to put these pictures somewhere safe, which I did after showing them to everyone I knew. On the first picture, Sabah handwrote: "To my darling Ramzy with my appreciation," and on the second she wrote: "With my appreciation," signed Sabah.

RAMZY BAROODY

Sabah hands me two autographed pictures during my visit to her apartment in Aley. This one she signed: "To dearest Ramzy with my appreciation-Sabah."

The Burning Cedars

*Second autographed picture from Sabah on
her boat holding a bottle of 7-UP,
by the Lebanese coastline.
This one she signed: "With love-Sabah."*

RAMZY BAROODY

The Burning Cedars

CHAPTER EIGHTEEN

THE POST INTERVIEW COMMENTARY

After meeting Sabah, uncle Tony thought it would be interesting to publish my take on the interview in his weekly column. The next day he sat me down with a list of questions concerning my thoughts about Sabah, my favorite song of hers and so on, which I was more than happy to answer. Little did I know that one of my answers almost got my uncle fired from his job.

The final question on the interview was: "whom do you like best, Sabah or Fairouz?" I answered bluntly and honestly "Sabah of course." Uncle Tony said that this was rather an unkind response so he re-worded it into, what he thought, a more politically correct fashion as follows:" For me, Sabah deserves a balcony seat while Fairouz belongs in the mezzanine."

Truthfully, although I was young and knew nothing about journalism, I believed that my answer was more "politically correct" than what he came up with but, after all, he was the experienced journalist and I was just a kid.

The following day after submitting the interview for review, uncle Tony was called into the publisher's office where he got an earful. Needless to say, that question along with the accompanying answer was never published.

Uncle Tony was too kind to tell me about the scolding he received that day, and I knew nothing about it till the following Friday when I tore through the magazine looking for my interview and realized that some of my answers had been re-worded or totally omitted. Personally, I didn't care about the revisions as long as I got to see my name and picture in print.

This was neither the first time, nor the last, that I would be mentioned in my uncles' weekly articles.

Uncle Tony devoted a monthly column in his articles especially for me and named it: "To my little love." In this column, he expressed his love and admiration for me, my likes and dislikes and various antics I performed around the house. Initially I was thrilled by this show of affection and admiration until it became a source of ridicule and mockery by school classmates, relatives and even my family especially my grandmother who teased me endlessly about it in her usual sarcastic sense of humor.

The Burning Cedars

CHAPTER NINETEEN

THE MILK AD

When I was seven, uncle Tony brought home a photographer to tell me that they wanted me for a milk commercial which was to be shown in movie theaters. They had me posing for the ad in front of a mosaic of the different Disney characters that were painted on a wall while holding a glass of milk and smiling. They then told me to drink from the glass and look into the camera and smile, and I happily complied. The ad pictures, that I still have today, turned out great and my favorite was the one of me posing with a milk moustache.

The following week, the whole family went to the theater to see my commercial, which was shown prior to the main movie. We sat in our seats and just before the movie started I looked up at the big screen and there I was, holding a glass of milk with a wide grin on my face. For weeks after that, I was the local celebrity in our village and wherever I went, women came up to me, pinched my cheeks and told me that they saw the commercial and how cute I was. I was a little uncomfortable with all the attention but it's all a part of being in show business, I thought to myself!

The Burning Cedars

My milk ad pictures were shown at several movie theaters making me somewhat of a local celebrity at the young age of seven.

RAMZY BAROODY

The Burning Cedars

CHAPTER TWENTY

THE CONCERT

*F*ree theater and concert tickets arrived to our house daily with requests for uncle Tony to attend and review the shows. For me, none were more exciting than the tickets to Sabah's new musical stage shows.

On a rainy evening, we piled into my dad's new Skylark and headed to Beirut to see Sabah's new show. As was customary with our family, we arrived half an hour late and were guided to our front row seats. Sabah was already on stage strutting around and singing. She was wearing a white flowing dress, which was rigged with dozens of small inconspicuous light bulbs. When she got to the verse of the song that called for the lights to be turned out, the hall went completely dark and her dress lit up like a Christmas tree. During intermission, Sabahs' sister came out into the audience heading directly towards my uncle: "Sabah was wondering why you came in late. You missed a good portion of the show," she said. My uncle explained that traffic was bad and apologized, assuring her that he would be able to write a favorable review of the show regardless.

Shortly after, Sabah came out for the second act during which she sang her famous song "Ya Dala3" which roughly translates to "The precious or cherished one."

Halfway through the song, she turns and points directly at me, not once, but twice.

By then, I had sunk so deep into my chair, I was almost on the floor. My mom kept jabbing me with her elbow telling me to look up and wave. "Nothing doing" I muttered. "Get up and look at her and smile" my mom continued as she grabbed me by my shirt collar and pulled me up. As I looked up, I realized that all eyes in the arena were on me.

I turned every shade of red as I freed myself from my mom's vice-like grip and sank deeper into my chair.

My uncle said that Sabah must've recognized me from our earlier meeting in her apartment, as she is known for remembering everything and everyone.

Furthermore, Sabah was a sharp-witted and skillful business and marketing woman who knew exactly which axes to grease to get what she wants. What better way to get a positive review from my uncle than to indulge his nephew in public display of affection and recognition.

For the next several months, my mom would ask me to re-enact the concert incident to everyone we knew, and I happily obliged. Outwardly I pretended to be embarrassed by all that attention yet I was full of glee and jubilation on the inside.

The Burning Cedars

Sabah recognized me during one of her concerts, pointing directly at me as I sank deeper into my seat which greatly embarrassed and delighted me!

RAMZY BAROODY

CHAPTER TWENTY-ONE

THE UNFULFILLED DREAM

*M*y mom had a beautiful voice and sang frequently around the house. Her voice closely resembled that of a famous Syrian-Egyptian singer named "Asmahan" who had died tragically in 1944 at the age of 32 by drowning in a canal outside of Cairo.

Asmahan had a turbulent personal life and an alleged espionage role in World War II, and it was rumored that her death was not accidental, yet no conclusive evidence emerged as to confirm or deny those rumors.

It had also been rumored that her main rival, Egyptian singer Umm Kulthum, was behind her death. Asmahan was the only female voice in Arab music to pose serious competition to that of Umm Kulthum, who was considered to be one of the Arab world's most distinguished singers of the 20th century.

In 1975, my uncle encouraged my mom to appear in a TV talent show named *Studio Al Fan* or *Talent Studio*. Performers from all over Lebanon and the Arab world competed on the show for their chance at stardom.

RAMZY BAROODY

On a cold January afternoon, my mom and uncle went to Beirut to appear on the show as we huddled around the TV anxiously awaiting her appearance.

Clearly nervous and shaking, my mom took the stage and performed her Asmahan rendition flawlessly, to thunderous applause. After the show, the producer took my mom aside and asked her candidly: "You have a beautiful voice but you need the proper training. I will sponsor you for the conservatoire where they will train your voice and teach you all the techniques of singing, but I have to ask you if you are willing to make the necessary sacrifices that come with fame. This path is full of thorns, and if you feel that you are not up for the task, you need to let me know now." My mom told him that she would get back to him in a few days as she pondered his advice.

The following day my mom was in a taxicab and overheard the driver saying to one of the passengers: "Did you see that woman who sang the Asmahan song last night. She sounded just like her. She is going to be famous." As soon as my mom exited the cab, she ran to a phone and called my uncle: "Call the producer and tell him I've decided to enroll in the conservatoire."

As soon as she hung up, she heard distant explosions and gunfire and saw everyone running for cover. She hurried back home, unaware that this was the beginning of a sixteen-year-long civil war which destroyed most of the country along with her dreams of becoming a famous singer.

The Burning Cedars

CHAPTER TWENTY-TWO

DAY ONE

I was in school on the day the war started. We could hear the gunfire in the distant from our classrooms and all the students and teachers hurried down to the cafeteria, which was partially underground with only a few rows of narrow windows high up above ground close to the ceiling. We were all at a loss as to exactly what was happening or how to get home. We heard on the radio that roads were impassable and shells were falling all around the capital. Suddenly, one of the teachers came up to me and told me that my uncle was waiting for me outside to take me home. I grabbed my heavy bookcase and ran outside and my uncle was sitting in his little Austin car waiting for me, clearly shaken up and upset.

He said fighting was erupting everywhere and most roads have been closed. To get home, we'd have to take the long way home through mountainous back roads passing through many Muslim and Druze villages. It took us several hours to get home safely and we gathered around the TV listening to the news. Militia fighters have taken over many neighborhoods and there were bloody massacres taking place along with house-to-house fighting. Beirut was divided into the Eastern Christian and the Western Muslim zones separated by

The Burning Cedars

what was called "the green line" where the fighting was the fiercest. Initially, the fighting was most intense during the night and would subside gradually at daybreak. Great apprehension and fear fell over the entire country, particularly in towns and villages where Christians and Muslims co-existed.

Our village, Alley, remained relatively calm yet tense during those initial months of the war. Gradually, more armed militia fighters were arriving to our village and roaming the streets and we knew that war was at our doorsteps.

For the first few months of the war, we were able to sporadically attend school on days when the fighting was minimal. Going through multiple checkpoints and back roads became the norm. However, returning home from school was a gamble as fighting would erupt again at anytime and we would get stranded. Some days, one hour into the school day and we would be sent home again. Eventually, school days became more infrequent until all schools were closed indefinitely.

I was eleven years old at the time and did not have a clear understanding of what was happening around me, especially since I have never been through a war. I could not fully grasp the concept of war or its consequences.

At a young age, one looks at life through a very narrow point of view, unable to clearly differentiate or understand the good from the bad or their significance. Although war terrified me, initially its direct impact on my life was a welcomed one. I had always dreaded school, and the war put an end to the strain I endured daily. I became to view the war as an extended vacation when I could stay home and feel safe and content. A few months passed when I quickly realized that war was an un-welcomed excuse to stay home from school. Our lives were in real jeopardy and people were dying all around us. Furthermore, fighting was no longer limited to downtown Beirut but had spread like wildfire throughout the country. One night we were jolted out of bed by a very bright light in the sky. No one knew what it was and we naively ran outside to investigate. When we got outside, the sky was dark except for the stars and a beautiful full moon. The moon was as big as I have ever seen it and the cool breeze made the stars shimmer in the night sky. As we were heading back indoors, we heard a distant boom of a cannon firing, and a very bright muffled explosion lit up the sky over our heads. We had never seen anything like it before but quickly realized that it was a Phosphorus bomb fired by the Christian militias from Beirut to aid them in visually inspecting and monitoring the movement of weapons and personnel in our village in preparation for an assault. In the following weeks and months, many more Phosphorous bombs lit up our night sky to be followed by an endless barrage of bombardment.

The Burning Cedars

CHAPTER TWENTY-THREE

THOSE RABBITS ARE OURS

*O*ne afternoon as the sun was going down, I was rounding up our chickens and guiding them to their coop for the evening. My brother was tending to our pigeons and my mom had just called us in for dinner when a loud explosion echoed through our village, followed by another, then another. The explosions continued for several hours at a steady pace. It turned out that the Druze militias had installed a huge cannon on the hill facing our village and were shelling the Christian towns across the valley.

Several minutes after the shelling started, the response came swiftly and violently and continued throughout the night. A target of particular interest to the Christian militias was our village city hall, which was unfortunately located directly across the street from our house and converted to the Druze militias' headquarters.

At one time I had mentioned to my uncle that I liked rabbits, and a few days later two fat black and white rabbits appeared. My uncle had bought them for me. I had no clue what to feed them or how to take care of them, but I loved them nevertheless. I figured if Bugs Bunny liked carrots, that's what I should be feeding these rabbits, but

The Burning Cedars

these two would not go near it. They ate lettuce plus anything they could gather in the backyard.

A few weeks later, the rabbits disappeared and I frantically looked everywhere for them. I had thought they must have run away and was sick over it until I happened to glance across the street and there they were, in a small cage on the steps of the town hall placed there by the militiamen who had stolen them from our backyard. I was furious and determined to get them back, so I marched up the long flight of steps into the city hall and confronted the militia soldiers: "Mister," I said to one of the soldiers, "These rabbits belong to me and I want them back." With a look of shock and, surprisingly, a little shame, he reached over and handed me back my rabbits. I grabbed my rabbits by their ears and jubilantly ran back home.

My family, especially my uncle, could not believe that I had the uncharacteristic nerve to walk up there and demand the return of my rabbits from those armed thugs, but were proud of me for doing so. Unfortunately, a few weeks later the rabbits disappeared again but this time for good.

Our next encounter with those same militiamen came a few weeks later, yet this time under much more serious and unpleasant circumstances.

RAMZY BAROODY

The Burning Cedars

CHAPTER TWENTY-FOUR

THE BLUE RADIO

During the war, electricity was almost non-existent, and we relied primarily on candlelight and battery powered radios to keep up with current events. A new electronic device that had arrived to Lebanon was the pocketsize transistor radio and I desperately wanted one. Uncle Tony came home one day with two wrapped gift boxes containing one red and one blue battery operated transistor radios.

I was overjoyed, and gave my brother the blue radio while keeping the red one. I loved my small palm-size radio and listened to it all day and night.

One Sunday afternoon my brother and I were in the TV room listening to our radios by the window, which faced the town hall when a group of armed militia men stormed the house, grabbed my brother and dragged him away. My mom became hysterical and was on the verge of another breakdown and, along with my dad, ran after them into the town city hall. Fearful for my brothers' life, they ran up and down the long and dark corridors screaming my brother's name then headed for the main office to inquire for his whereabouts.

They were told that he had been locked up in one of the jail cells. The militia commander explained that they had seen my brother in the window holding a walky-talky and relaying strategic information to the Christian militias in Beirut. My parents were shocked by this misinformation, explaining that all he had was a transistor radio used to listen to music and news, but they wouldn't hear of it. They insisted on detaining my brother overnight for a full investigation. My parents refused to leave my brother alone and camped outside his prison cell till the following morning, sleeping on the cold bare floor. The following morning, one of the militiamen recognized my dad as an old school mate: "What are you doing here?" he inquired. "My son Shucry has been detained for spying" my dad answered frantically, "Please do something to help us."

The militia guy then ran into the office and was heard saying, "I know these people. His father was Dr. Shucry Baroody and they have no involvement in anything. Let his son go right now." A few minutes later he returned with two other men and unlocked my brothers' holding cell: "Take your son and go home," he said urgently to my parents. With all the chaos and mayhem taking place during that time, anyone of an opposing religion on either side could be kidnapped, jailed or killed for just being in the wrong place at the wrong time. As one of the handful of Christian families remaining in Aley, it was short of a miracle that we had not been harmed by the lawless militias in control of the village or that no physical harm came to my brother that night.

Our detriment would come a few months later not from the Druze militias, but ironically from the Christian militias of Beirut.

The Burning Cedars

CHAPTER TWENTY-FIVE

JEHOVAH'S WITNESSES

My mother has always been a religious person who read the bible daily and lived by its commandments. She was born into the Roman Catholic religion but saw little redemption in it. She sought the teachings of many religious denominations including the Protestants, Presbyterians, Baptists, and Methodists but none appealed to her.

In the summer of 1976, during a respite in the fighting, a woman by the name of Lucille Marina came to our door. After a brief discussion with my mother, Lucille came into the house and they headed for the TV room. During their conversation, I listened at the door and heard talk about "Jesus" and "God" and "redemption" so I lost interest and headed out to play. The woman stayed for several hours and as she exited, assured my mother that she would return the following day to continue the conversation. A few minutes later I snuck back into the TV room and looked through some magazines the woman had left behind, the first was "The Watchtower" and the other "Awake." Below the title the magazines declared, "Announcing the Kingdom of Jehovah." I had never heard of this religion nor did I give it much thought at the time.

The Burning Cedars

The following day around the same time, Lucille came back with a bag full of publications, magazine and a couple of bibles. On that day they were joined by my brother.

Lucille eventually became a regular at our house, to the detestation and admonishment of my grandmother, who tried unsuccessfully to put a stop to Lucille's visits.

My grandmother ridiculed Lucille, nicknamed her "Lucy show" and expressed her displeasure with her visits, but Lucille was un-deterred.

One cold winter afternoon, Lucille was conducting a bible study with my mother and brother in the TV room, which was the only heated room in the house. My grandmother claimed that she was cold and insisted on taking her afternoon nap on the couch in that room during the bible study. Halfway through the study, my "sleeping" grandmother let out the longest, loudest, and smelliest fart she could muster. Gasping for air, everyone stampeded out of the room as my grandmother calmly continued her alleged nap.

Choosing a religion of her own accord without the influence of others gave my mom the self-determination and control she desperately longed for in her life. Choices were always made for her and for the first time, she got to express her unique wishes and desires that have so far eluded her in life.

Both my mother and brother saw in the Jehovah's Witnesses a clear departure from all the other Christian denominations, a difference they liked and approved of: "Other than some basic and minor differences, most Christian denominations are basically the same" my mom used to say, justifying her devotion to the Witnesses and defending her decision to her un-approving family and friends.

At the time, we were unable to explain my dad's unconditional approval of my mom's decision to join the Witnesses. Although he never personally became involved, he actively encouraged and supported my mom with her new faith.

It later dawned on us that Jehovah Witnesses do not observe any holidays or birthdays and therefore, there's no need for gift giving on holidays or birthdays.
My dad wholeheartedly approved of this since now, he had a legitimate excuse to be the Grinch of Christmas.

Jehovah's Witnesses are by and large good honest people with a noteworthy message, a plausible interpretation of the bible and a deep devotion to their religion.

For some time, I was curious about their views and attended meetings with my mother and brother on a regular basis. I did not, however, advance past that initial curiosity stage.

Once you become a witness, you must strictly adhere to what is viewed as acceptable behavior by the elders based on their interpretations of the bible and any deviation, however small, is grounds for immediate disfellowship. That level of control and oversight alarms many outsiders and is behind the misconception by some that this religion is more of a cult.

Witnesses also emphasize to their members the need to leave the "outside" world behind once you join and to only associate with other witnesses.

The Burning Cedars

Associating with friends or family members outside the religion is discouraged. Probably the best-known fact about the witnesses is their door-to-door witnessing obligation. As a matter of fact, door-to-door visits are not optional, rather mandatory and a witness must log his or her service hours "in the field" daily and those hours are tallied and forwarded to their headquarters outside of New York city monthly.

In 1977, my brother became a baptized Jehovah's Witness followed the following year by my mother. It was a particularly violent day in the fighting and bombs were falling all around us when my mother got baptized in the bathtub of the same people who would later that year take us in when, by nothing short of a miracle, we survived a direct assault on our house which left it in a virtual ruin.

My mother being baptized as a Jehovah's Witness in 1978.

Lucy Marina, the woman who converted my mother and brother into Jehovah Witnesses.

The Burning Cedars

CHAPTER TWENTY-SIX

THERE WAS BLOOD EVERYWHERE

The war raged on as conditions continued to deteriorate throughout the country. Electricity and water had been none existent for some time, but now food was becoming scarce as well.

Although we had a good supply of chickens in the backyard, no one had the heart or the know-how to slaughter them. Finally, out of necessity and hunger, my dad had to ask one of the neighbors to do the job for us and in return, he gave him one chicken for each one he killed.

The constant bombardment made us feel very unsafe in our home, but even if we had wanted to leave, conditions were so traitorous everywhere that no place was safe. Furthermore, my dad said that if we left, militias would take over the building and we would have no home to return to. We came to the decision that the dining room was the safest place in the house to take shelter, and that was where we spent most of our days and nights.

We ventured out only sporadically to get supplies and use the bathroom. Our dining room was in the rear of the house facing the back walls of the stores my dad had built and rented.

The Burning Cedars

On a Sunday afternoon in 1978, and after a particularly violent night of shelling and counter-shelling, the fighting had finally let-up and my dad decided to venture out to investigate where the bombs had fallen the night before.

Some fell so close to our house that metal shrapnels littered our backyard while others broke several windows in the hallway. Against my mothers' wishes, I naively followed my dad outside accompanied by my brother.

We had barely made it across the street when the Christian militias from Beirut launched an onslaught with a series of about a dozen bombs that fell all around us in succession. In horror, we scattered and ran toward the house with my dad and brother making it in first. The noise was so loud that all I could hear was ringing in my ears and the whizzing noise of shrapnels as they flew past me. As I was running I felt a very warm sensation on my back, which jolted me with such a force that I was pushed to the ground landing on my side in the middle of the street. I looked up and in the distant was my mother standing in the doorway of our house screaming in terror. I was unable to hear or speak and could not interpret the expression on my mother's face nor what she was trying to say to me. I remember screaming "oh my God," as the bombs continued to fall and I was unable to get out of harm's way, I thought this would be the last time I would see her. I tried to get back on my feet but I was disoriented and unsure in which direction to run. The terrible smell of sulfur filled the air and got more intense with each blast as the bombs continued to rain down on us. They say people who have experienced life-threatening situations and extreme stress and panic, describe their ordeal as if watching the events around them unfold in slow motion, like watching a protracted movie, with little or no associated emotions or feelings in those fleeting moments. That day, as I lied on the hot asphalt, I understood. Suddenly I felt someone pick me up and carry me over his shoulders as he ran towards the house. It was uncle Tony. Once we made it inside, I slowly turned to him and smiled thinking that all was well now, but I was shocked by what I saw. He was soaked in blood and looked at me in a way I have never seen from him before. I then realized that the blood covering him was my own.

The Burning Cedars

CHAPTER TWENTY-SEVEN

AM I GOING TO DIE?

My uncle sat me down in a chair in the hallway as everyone gathered around yelling and screaming in terror. I was lightheaded and confused and the voices around me were muffled and incomprehensible. Through the crowd, an unfamiliar face was standing in the doorway. He asked if we needed assistance. He was a local villager who happened to be driving by and saw all the turmoil and mayhem taking place: "my car is outside and I can take your son to the hospital" he told my parents. My uncle quickly carried me to the mans' old Mercedes which, apparently, he had been using as a taxicab and everyone crammed inside as we sped to the local hospital. I sat in the middle of the back seat and my mom was on my right. My uncle and brother on the other side of me and my dad in the front along with the drive.

A few blocks from our house a residential building had been converted into a makeshift hospital to treat the daily influx of the injured and dying. Driving at sixty, we made the sharp left turn uphill towards the hospital. As the driver made the turn at high speed, my mom's car door opened and she went flying out into the street landing

The Burning Cedars

on the pavement. The driver immediately stopped and we looked back and saw my mom lifting her head off the pavement yelling "keep going, keep going" but my dad would not hear of it.

Bruised and bleeding from both knees, my mom hobbled back and got into the car and we continued on our way. We arrived at the hospital and two doctors placed me on a stretcher and, with no electricity, had to carry me up the steep flight of steps to the third floor. All the windows had been sandbagged and the rooms were dark and smelled of blood and disinfectant. The hallways were lined with dozens of the injured and dying, some laid there speechless while others screamed in agony.

"His injuries are too severe to be treated here" the doctor said, "we need to take him to a hospital in Beirut." "How are we going to do that?" my dad inquired, "it's too dangerous and all the main roads are blocked and impassable."

The doctor explained that they will transport me in an ambulance, and will be allowed to go through the blockades and the checkpoints. They will also have to take the back roads down the mountain that are relatively sheltered from bombardment.

They placed temporary bandages on my wounds to control the bleeding and loaded me into the ambulance. My mom and dad got into the back of the ambulance with me and my brother and uncle Tony headed home.

The ride to Beirut took us close to two hours and we finally arrived at the American University Hospital, where I was immediately transferred to the basement which was turned into an emergency room, lined with hundreds of beds filled with the injured and maimed. I was stretched out on one of the beds on my back looking up at the cement ceiling, unable to sit up or turn over. All through the night I laid there listening to the moans and the distressing cries for help from everyone around me, as my mom and dad sat by my side holding my hand. As I could not see my injuries or feel much pain, I contemplated the extent of my plight as I drifted in and out of consciousness.

Around dawn the following morning, I was finally wheeled into the emergency room and the doctors wanted to take some x-rays of my head, torso, and legs. An hour later, they came back with a concerned look on their faces wanting to take more x-rays.

"Am I going to die?" I asked my mother. Clearly disturbed by my question, she answered: "I will not let you die." She said it over and over again as she massaged my blood-encrusted hands.

The Burning Cedars

CHAPTER TWENTY-EIGHT

DIAGNOSIS

The doctors finally returned with the results of the x-rays: "He has two shrapnels lodged in his cranium, two deep in his back next to his heart and lungs and as you can see" pointing at my left leg "a sizeable chunk of his left thigh has been torn out by a large shrapnel. We will try our best, but cannot guarantee that we will be able to save his left leg as the wound is large and very deep." Immediately my mom and dad began sobbing at the news but I showed little emotion yet I was startled and numb.

My parents were asked to leave the operating room and the doctors went to work on my leg first. So far I had felt little to no pain but now, as the doctors began digging into my leg, I felt as if someone had inserted a knife into my body and lit it on fire. I cried out in pain but the doctor told me to remain calm as they removed the chunks of metal embedded deep in my thigh and tried to salvage my leg.

At one point, the pain got so intense that I could not hold back the tears and I tried to sit up but got very lightheaded from all the loss of blood.

The Burning Cedars

Several hours went by as the pain level continued to escalate. As they were sowing my leg back together, the deep penetrating stabbing pain of the needles was too much to endure and I passed out.

I came to as the doctors were bandaging my head after removing several metal shrapnels from my skull. After I was wheeled out of the operating room, the doctors explained to my parents the extent of my injuries: "We were able to save his leg but had the wound been less than a quarter inch deeper, it would've severed a major artery and he would have either bled to death or we would've had to cut off his leg.

They continued: "Three shrapnels are still imbedded in his scull but they have just missed his brain. We are not removing them as it is a delicate operation and could make things worse. They will not cause any further damage. Most likely in a few years the body will slowly expel them toward the surface where they may be removed. The remaining two shrapnels in his back are to be left there indefinitely. They pose no danger to his health and the body will likely seal them in place with a layer of fat."

RAMZY BAROODY

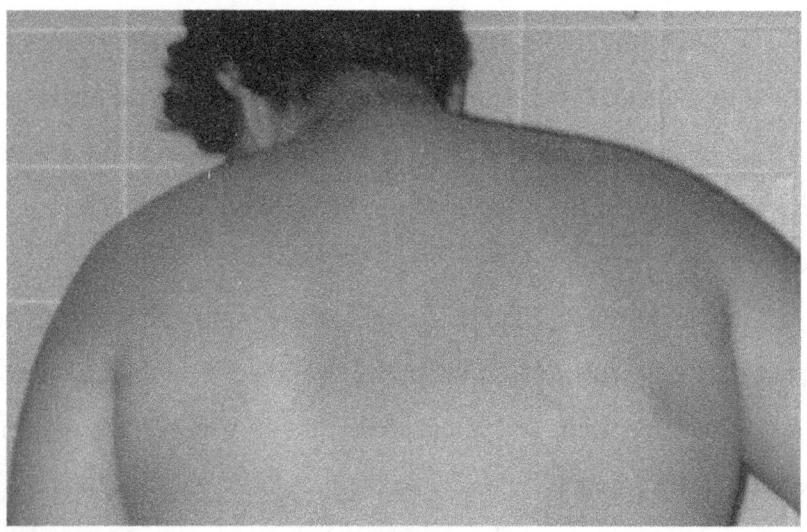

Ten years after I was badly injured, the entrance wound remained clearly visible where the two shrapnels tore into my back (below right shoulder) and lodged themselves into a layer of fat less than an inch from my lungs.

Three more are imbedded in my skull while the largest tore away almost half of my upper left thigh.

The Burning Cedars

CHAPTER TWENTY-NINE

MY THREE AUNTS

*T*wo days after arriving at the hospital, I was released and headed home. Prior to leaving, the doctors gave my mom specific instructions on how to care for my wounds to prevent infection and speed up the healing process. The ambulance driver drove like a madman on the same traitorous roads up the mountain to Aley. It was late in the afternoon and roads became increasingly dangerous at night as artillery shells fell indiscriminately and snipers took aim at anything that moved. When we got home, we were surprised to see my three aunts, my mothers' sisters, waiting to welcome us home.

I greatly loved my aunts as they were equally warm, kind, and caring. The youngest aunt Mona, a vivacious woman always with a smile on her face. She liked and was liked by everyone and had great charisma and positive energy. She married an equally kind man who worked as a taxi driver, and they had three boys.

Aunt Violet was the quiet type, yet equally as kind and down to earth as her sisters. Prior to getting married, she worked as a

The Burning Cedars

kindergarten schoolteacher. For one summer, my parents enrolled me in her class, mostly because I was bored at home.

Disciplining children was not Aunt Violets' forte and her kindergarten class was totally chaotic and disorderly.

Aunt Wadad was the toughest of the three sisters. She worked for years in the telephone company and married an army man whom she knew little about and liked even less. She often told us that on her wedding day as she walked down the aisle, she almost ran out of the church and thought to herself "What am I doing to myself?" It later turned out that her intuition was correct. The two of them never got along and argued constantly. In 1976 during the height of the war, aunt Waddad's husband left her in the middle of the night and moved to Brazil. She was left alone with three small children.

The worst of it is that several years later, when he came back because, as he put it, things did not work out for him in Brazil, she took him back. She justified her actions by saying that the children needed a father and she had no other choice. Aunt Wadad was under a tremendous amount of stress trying to raise three young children during the war, and even though she detested her husband, his presence must have given her a sense of security and a little comfort knowing that she would not have to raise the children alone. The two of them are still together today although they hardly communicate. He spends most of his time in their summer home in the mountains while she's in their Beirut apartment.

*(**Top**) Aunt Wadad (left) with Aunt Mona and her two sons visiting an old historic fort outside of Beirut.*

Aunt Violet with her youngest son

Aunt Wadad with husband during happier times

The Burning Cedars

CHAPTER THIRTY

THE OLD ATTIC WAS LIFTED OFF ITS FOUNDATION

I spent the next few months recovering at home while the mayhem continued outside. My dad remained adamant against leaving insisting that the war will end soon.

In August of 1978, three months after I was injured, I had just finished my lunch which consisted of wheat germ (bulgur) cooked with chicken and chicken stock.

I was resting on my mattress in the dining room waiting for my mom to clean my wounds and change the bandages. My brother was sitting in his chair next to me reading his Bible. My grandmother Zafer had left the country several months prior and was staying with her sister in South Carolina.

My grandmother's sister, Salwa, met and married her husband, Naseeb, in the 1940s in Lebanon and they immigrated to the US. They settled in Florence, South Carolina where they owned a Budweiser beer distribution company.

As my mom was getting ready to attend to my injuries, my dad headed for his bedroom for an afternoon nap. He felt relatively safe sleeping in his bed that day since we have not received much shelling

The Burning Cedars

since earlier that morning. My dad usually naps several hours every afternoon, but on that day, he could not fall asleep and after only half an hour, got back up and walked over to the dining room to join us.

As soon as he entered the room, a tremendous explosion shook the entire house, and dust and the smell of gunpowder was everywhere. Above the dining room was an attic with a balcony overlooking the room. When we were kids, we used to climb up into that attic and rummage through the many antiques stored there by my grandparents.

Dusty old chairs, pictures, painting of old relatives, tables, rugs, and many other items, covered in cobwebs had been stored there and forgotten.

My most valuable find in that attic was my grandfathers' old medical leather case, which he carried around during house visits. It contained a stethoscope, needles, tongue depressors, and a medical reference book along with his appointment journal. In his journal, my grandfather jotted down the names of his clients, diagnosed ailment, time and date of the visit and his fee, if any. In our village, my grandfather was notorious for his generosity and kindheartedness, and his appointment book clearly reflected this. Next to many of his clients' names in the "Fee" column, he had scribbled a "Zero."

When my dad walked into the dining room on that day after his short nap, and the explosion took place, I saw that attic and its' balcony, the place where I spent many hours role playing and imagining what life must've been like when my grandfather was alive, lift up off its foundation and settle back down several feet forward. The dust was so thick that we could not see one another and only heard coughing and gasping for air.

Shortly after the dust began to settle, in total shock and almost blind by the flying dust and debris, unable to hear from the loud explosion, we looked around visually inspecting each other and realized that uncle Tony was not in the room with us. My dad began to frantically yell: "Tony, Tony."

A few seconds went by with no response and my dad called for my uncle again in desperation. Out of the dust and haze, a muffled noise cried out from the next room "I'm ok." My uncle then emerged from the cloud of dirt and gunpowder, white as a ghost, covered in powder from head to toe.

He had been in his room, which is adjacent to my dad's room, getting dressed and the explosion toppled his closet on top of him pinning him to the ground under its weight. This most likely saved his life and he was able to squirm his way out from under it and feel his way back to the dining room with nothing more than minor scratches and a good dowsing of white powder from the flying debris.

It was eerily quiet for several minutes as we all stood immobilized in place. Shells usually fell two or three at a time in rapid succession and we waited for another round, which luckily did not come. My dad walked back toward the dining room door and peeked out into the hallway which separated the dining room from my parents' bedroom. "OH MY GOD" he yelled.

A mortar shell had entered my parent's bedroom through the window and exploded in the middle of the room pulverizing

The Burning Cedars

everything. It left a huge crater in the floor and a large hole in the wall of the hallway.

My dad then screamed: "All our money is in that room, in one of my suit pockets."

Everything in that room had been reduced to a fine gray powder, including the beds, the dressers and the closet where his suit with the money hung. My dad then ran into the bedroom through the hole in the wall as my mom followed, pleading with him to get out. He hysterically stepped over the piles of dust and debris heading towards where his closet with the money used to be and began digging through the rubble with his bare hands.

Nothing was discernable in the room except for a large crater in the middle of the floor surrounded by piles of dark gray ash. My mom then tried to reason with him, pointing out that the intense explosion had melted the metal bed frames, and that in no way the jacket or the money could've survived such tremendous heat. My dad refused to give up and continued to sift through the rubble with his hands, scooping up the dirt then letting it run through his fingers.

While my dad hysterically searched, we quickly gathered a few of our belongings, preparing to somehow get away from this destruction and chaos. We did not know where to go or how to get there but we could not stay in the house. We headed for the back kitchen door as my mom went back into the bedroom to fetch my dad. As I walked out of the dining room, debris floating in the air was beginning to settle back down.

I looked through the crater in my parent's bedroom wall and saw one piece of paper gently meandering through the air. I looked closer and noticed it was one of my dad's currency notes, half burnt, floating calmly through the air like an injured and bewildered butterfly.

The note, still smoldering by the intense heat, had a picture of the Lebanese cedar tree on one side which was almost completely burnt by the explosion and I thought to myself, how fitting that this peace of paper can foretell the future of my country!

We briskly walked to the back door and for a minute, there was total silence in the bedroom followed by cries of joy and disbelief. My dad had reached down into one of the piles and pulled up his sports jacket: "I found it" he screamed, "and the money is still intact inside the pocket."

Finding a stack of paper money among piles of rubble was nothing short of a miracle. Metal and wood had been reduced to ash yet his money lingered unscathed.

His life savings has miraculously been spared by the inferno that disintegrated everything in its path and holding on to his jacket for dear life, he stumbled out of the room and headed for the kitchen where we had gathered.

The Burning Cedars

My grandmother Zafer (right) with her brother-in-law Naseeb Baroody and her sister Salwa in Florence, South Carolina. At the first sign of hostilities in Lebanon, my grandmother was on a plane to South Carolina leaving us behind to endure the violence and blood shed.

RAMZY BAROODY

From the smoldering ash, my dad retrieves his life-savings, including this one pound (Lira) note which survived the inferno that destroyed and melted everything in its path. Over thirty five years later, the smell of sulfur endures on this currency, a grim reminder of its past.

The Burning Cedars

CHAPTER THIRTY-ONE

A DARING ESCAPE

We headed for the back door with no idea of where to go or how to get there. All of a sudden I felt sick to my stomach and threw up my entire dinner.

Our kitchen was below street level and we had to climb up a flight of steps to get to the street. I looked up and a tall thin man stood at the top of the stairs: "I heard the explosion and was coming in to see if you needed help," he said.

"A bomb entered the house and we need to get out now," my dad replied. The man said that his car was parked outside and he will take us anywhere we wanted to go. Two miracles in one day were too much to hope for, yet this man was undeniably a Godsend.

Back in those days and having lived in a small village all of our lives, even with a raging bloody and vicious war, people still looked out for each other and helped one another in times of need. Twice now we had been rescued by local Druze villagers who were putting their lives in harm's way to help us. We decided to go to a nearby village which was relatively safe because of its location, tucked away on the far side of the mountain, unreachable by the shelling from Beirut.

The Burning Cedars

Months earlier, my mother had been baptized as a Jehovah's Witness in the bathtub of a nice couple who lived in that village, and we decided to stay with them for a few days until we decide on our next course of action. When we got there, the couple was sitting outside and upon seeing us, their jaws almost dropped to the ground.

After the explosion, our primary mission was to leave the house, unconcerned by our appearances. My mom had slipped on a pair of red high-heeled shoes while in her nightgown, and my brother and I were in our pajamas. Both my dad and uncle were totally covered with white powdery dust, looking more like ghosts than human beings.

The couple we stayed with was very nice and welcoming, and even though we could hear the shells falling in the distant, we knew that for the time being, we were relatively safe. After several days, we had to face the fact that we can neither go back home, nor continue imposing on our friends for much longer.

My dad decided that the only plausible solution to our predicament is to leave the country. We will go to Egypt where my aunt Grace and her family had been living since the beginning of the war. This long-awaited announcement was music to everyone's ears.

RAMZY BAROODY

The Burning Cedars

CHAPTER THIRTY-TWO

PLANNING OUR ESCAPE

The war raged on and getting out of the country was a difficult and dangerous undertaking. The airport had been closed for some time and the only exit routes were either through Syria or Cyprus. The roads leading to Syria were extremely dangerous and news of abductions and killings were publicized daily. Furthermore, there were no guarantees that while in Syria we would be able to travel to Egypt.

Cyprus is a large Greek/Turkish island in the Mediterranean Sea, 108 kilometers (67 miles) off the coast of Lebanon. During the war, a ferry transported those fleeing the fighting to the island on a regular basis from ports in Beirut and Jounieh to the north. Due to the extremely volatile situation and the uncertainty associated with traveling through either Syria or Cyprus, my dad decided to search for another route that would take us directly to Egypt.

A few days later, we learned of a ship that sailed weekly from the port of Sidon in the south of Lebanon to Alexandria in Egypt. This was our best escape route so we packed up what little we could salvage from the house, rented a taxi and traveled the fifty kilometers, or about thirty-one miles to the city of Sidon. Once we got there, we were dismayed to learn that the designated vessel for the trip was actually a large cargo ship.

By that time, however, there was no turning back so we unloaded our bags and headed for the dock. Hundreds of people lined up to get onboard and we joined them, standing in line for several hours waiting. The injured and maimed got on first, followed by women with children, then families. We were horded like cattle to the upper deck of the ship where everyone scrambled to claim an area to settle down on, using blankets laid out over the bare metal deck for warmth.

Those who got on first claimed the outer perimeter of the deck while we were squeezed into the center, surrounded by hundreds of people, unable to move around or stretch our legs.

Our location on deck turned out to be a blessing in disguise, for what was about to take place mid-voyage during that night was nothing short of a horror story in itself.

The Burning Cedars

CHAPTER THIRTY-THREE

ONBOARD THE CARGO SHIP

The ship left port around five pm that day and was expected to arrive in Alexandria, Egypt early the next morning. I was so exhausted physically and mentally that as soon as the ship set sail, I passed out on the cold steel deck. Around midnight, we were awakened by the sudden halt of the ship and heard a loud commotion upfront. We saw a group of about five men in army uniforms walking around the deck with flashlights looking for something or someone.

The elderly man next to us whispered that the Israeli navy had intercepted and stopped the ship. Israeli navy men had boarded the ship looking for Palestinian fighters and ammunition. We may not be allowed to continue to Egypt, rather diverted to Israel or even back to Beirut. The men searched the ship for several hours while Israeli war ships circled our ship shining bright flood lights onboard and all around.

As abruptly as this incident had started, the Israeli men quickly got back onboard their vessel and we were allowed to proceed. "What else could possibly go wrong?" I asked my dad. Famous last words as that fateful night dragged on. Around three am, the ship sailed head on into one of the most violent storms I have ever seen.

The Burning Cedars

Twenty to thirty foot waves smashed into the hull of the ship tipping it violently from side to side. The skies opened up with torrential downpours along with nonstop lighting and deafening thunder. As each wave slammed into the ship, it created a chilling cavernous resonance from the empty belly of this cargo vessel.

At first, luggage and clothing were dragged overboard and into the violent sea by the force of each wave and we later learned that several people on the perimeter of the deck were swept into the sea as well.

Throughout all this, the ship seemed like it was meandering around with no clear direction or heading. It was tossed around like a toy boat in circles with each wave. Several young men decided that they wanted to confront the captain and when they broke into the control room, they found him stooped over the wheel uselessly drunk. They became so furious that they beat him back to soberness, forcing him to take control of the wheel and guiding the ship back onto its correct course toward Alexandria. Two pm the next day, I was resting with my head on my mom's lap. No one had gotten any sleep the night before and we were all exhausted and totally drained.

All of a sudden, a wave of cheering and clapping trickled from the front of the ship, gradually getting louder as people stood up and began to jump up and down. I propped myself up holding on to my mother's arm and there, in the distant, bathed in the warm Egyptian sunshine on the shores of the blue Mediterranean, was the city of Alexandria. We finally arrived safely in Egypt.

RAMZY BAROODY

The Burning Cedars

CHAPTER THIRTY-FOUR

THE ROAD TO CAIRO

*W*e arrived in Alexandria in the middle of September, 1978. It was a beautiful sunny day as palm trees swayed in the distant and the warm Egyptian sun bathed the shores of the blue Mediterranean.

The ship docked safely and we hurriedly gathered our water soaked belongings, rushing towards the exit. Taxis were lined up waiting for fares so we jumped into the first available cab and told the driver that we wanted to go to Cairo.

"Cairo?" he inquired, "Do you know that it is 230 kilometers (145 miles) away?"

"Yes" my dad answered, when in reality we had no idea of the vast distance between the two cities. The cab driver reluctantly agreed to take us after settling on the fare with my dad. We had not eaten since leaving Beirut, so my dad asked the driver if we could stop somewhere to get an authentic Egyptian meal: "Here's a Mango stand," the driver pointed out "You can't get any more authentic than that.

How about grabbing some mangos to hold you over till we get to Cairo?" Mangos for dinner was not quite what we had in mind but we were starving and the driver did not seem too eager to waste time, so we pulled over and my dad purchased a bag of Mangos from the roadside stand.

As we drove off, the driver pulled out a Swiss army knife from the glove compartment: "Let's have a taste," he said as my mom peeled a couple and passed them around to everyone. Mango bits and juice dripped everywhere but the drive did not seem concerned about that. Instead, he asked: "So, how was your trip?!"

The Burning Cedars

CHAPTER THIRTY-FIVE

LOOKING TO UNWIND

We had finally managed to leave our war-torn country, and for the past three years, our entire survival was reduced to the perceived protective walls of a dark and cold backroom while bombs exploded all around us while we huddled in fear and trepidation of what may come. It was difficult to comprehend that somewhere else in the world, life went on as usual, and people were living a normal life.

Now, on our way to Cairo, we passed villages of farmers tending their livestock by the canals, kids climbing up trees to harvest fruit, street vendors on the side of the road selling dates, mangos and papaya and, as we got closer to Cairo, the congested roads and outdoor eateries were a welcomed site.

It was almost nighttime when we arrived outside Aunt Grace's apartment in the upscale Cairo suburb of Zamalek. The street was lined with trees on both sides and hundreds of birds getting ready to roost for the night chirped loudly as they flew from one branch to the next, squeezing each other out to claim their nesting area.

We exited the taxi and walked up the steps to my aunts' second floor apartment. After receiving a lukewarm welcome, as was customary with my aunt, we were shown to our rooms.

The Burning Cedars

I shared the bedroom with my two younger cousins, my uncle slept in the middle room with my two older cousins, and my mom and dad slept in my aunt's room while she slept on the couch in the living room.

Since the apartment was so large, we did not feel as if we were imposing or inconveniencing anyone by temporarily staying there. My aunt, however, felt otherwise and within a few days of our arrival, she began dropping hints that we should begin looking for our own apartment. After one week, she took my mom aside and insisted that we find our own place as soon as possible. My dad had been looking at several apartments and decided to rent a lovely two bedroom furnished ground floor apartment a few blocks away from my aunt.

We quickly packed and moved to our new place which, for us, was the perfect apartment on a lovely street, full of shops and restaurants in the heart of the Zamalek area.

For the first few weeks, our transition to a new country was numbing and insipid. We had just left a war zone, came close to dying onboard a freight ship in the middle of a raging sea, uncertain of the length of time we would have to stay in Egypt, all unraveled our nerves and drained us of all vigor or feelings.

For years now we have lived everyday facing traumatic and life threatening experiences. We have learned to cope by living in denial to escape, creating a fantasy world in our minds which acted as a buffer between fantasy and reality. It was our minds' self defense mechanism to help maintain our sanity. Days and months seemed to blend together into a vaguely recollected memory, fuzzy and scrambled. Once we removed ourselves from such an environment, all those suppressed feelings and emotions bubbled up to the surface, flooding and overwhelming us, almost paralyzing us physically for some time until we were able to gradually sort and compartmentalize them, and gradually, this flood of emotions began to subside.

We never considered settling in Egypt permanently, yet as the war in Lebanon raged on, we were grateful to be out of the country and able to take this time to relax and unwind. After all we have endured, seen and heard during the war, relaxation was an art we had to re-learn slowly. We were a bundle of nerves, ready to react and jump out of our seats at the first sound of a slamming door, a loud car or a passing thunderstorm. Eventually we settled in and calmed down, deciding that we are to enjoy our stay in Egypt and worry less about what the future may hold for us, at least for the next several months.

The Burning Cedars

CHAPTER THIRTY-SIX

NEW EXPERIENCES

Arabic is the official language of Egypt and with some slight differences in the dialect, we had no difficulty in that regard. Nonetheless, in this predominantly Muslim country, the culture, associations, food, holidays and almost every facet of day-to-day living is greatly influenced and guided by Islamic religious beliefs, reducing the values and liberties of minorities to mere inconveniences, which they reluctantly endured.

Unlike Lebanon, Egypt is mostly desert and extremely over-populated. Close to ninety percent of the population live in extreme poverty while the remaining ten percent thrive in wealth and opulence, with no middle class to speak of. These factors combine to fashion a society of haves and have-nots, equally contributing to the grime and pollution of their towns and cities.

In Cairo, street beggars are on every corner and unsanitary conditions, dirty air and over-congested streets make for an industrious yet wonderful city.

Every morning, the trash collector came by our house to haul away the garbage. He was an elderly man riding on a cart pulled by two donkeys. In the cart where the garbage was collected rode his

The Burning Cedars

three young sons, rummaging through the trash for discarded food and clothing.

When you purchased a soda bottle you always held it up to the light to make sure there were no "floaters" in it, possibly a cockroach or ants. The newspaper reported daily on the unsanitary conditions, especially in the food and water. A front-page headline stated that a bat had been found in a loaf of bread, along with pictures to prove it.

My mom has always been germ phobic, and the unhygienic and polluted surroundings elevated her phobia into an acute state of paranoia. She washed her hands constantly and sanitized everything she came in contact with.

If she needed to cut an apple, she washed her hands first, then the apple, then the knife and the dish, cut the apple, the wash the knife again, then her hands. It was the norm in our house for fruits and vegetables to taste like soap! My brother complained constantly that his favorite fruit, grapes, tasted like eating dishwashing detergent. This is because my mom got in the habit of soaking grapes in water and soap for hours prior to serving them.

She vacuumed, mopped and sanitized the house daily and while most homes smelled of cooking or fresh flowers, ours constantly smelled of bleach.

Several weeks into our stay, we hired a maid who took care of the food shopping, cooked our meals and cleaned the apartment (with close supervision by my mother who, on most days, did more cleaning than the maid). The maid was a sweet middle-aged woman whom I used to joke with constantly, making fun of her Egyptian dialect. I would recite bad words I've learned and she would say, "That's not a good word" and "You shouldn't be saying that," but I would say it again until she starts to laugh, knowing that I am teasing her.

Several months into her employment, my mom noticed that the dinners the maid cooked were lacking several ingredients and portions were gradually becoming smaller. In particular, the meat portions were tiny along with several other ingredients that were at times completely missing.

After the maid left for the market one morning, my mom went through her bag and found pieces of meat, vegetables and other food items she had planned to sneak out of the house. Upon hearing the news, my dad insisted that we should immediately fire the maid. My mom, on the other hand, being her kind and loving self, rejected the idea. She justified the maid's actions as those of a poor and hungry woman trying to feed her family.

We were shocked by my righteous mothers' justification of stealing, but she insisted that she will not let this woman or her family go hungry. So the maid stayed and nothing was said to her about why our meals kept getting smaller and smaller.

Egypt enjoys a warm climate year-round, sustaining many exotic and tropical fruits and vegetables, grown and cultivated by the Nile river shores and its many man-made canals.

A favorite of my parents are *dates*, sweet fruit, dark purple/brown in color when ripe that grow on palm trees in large bunches. Individually, a date is shaped like a long narrow finger about five inches in length.

The Burning Cedars

My mom was particularly fond of dates and instructed the maid to purchase a jar of the fruit on one of her market runs. The maid returned with a large jar of pitted dates and my mom quickly took one out and bit into it. She noticed that the date was exceptionally crunchy and tasted a little odd. As she looked at the uneaten portion in her hand, she saw wings and hind legs. It was a huge cockroach that had been pickled in with the dates.

Leaping into the air, she ran straight for the bathroom. I was concerned that she would use soap and bleach to rinse out her mouth, but the noises emanating from the bathroom suggested otherwise.

RAMZY BAROODY

The Burning Cedars

CHAPTER THIRTY-SEVEN

LANDMINES AND CRAZY DOGS

We spent most of our time in Egypt relaxing or hanging out with my cousins. We visited dozens of ancient landmarks such as the pyramids, temples and tombs, went to museums, saw mommies, shopped at the open-air markets and took day trips with my cousins exploring different areas of the country. My parents met other Lebanese couples that they visited almost daily and went to dinners with nightly. My mom and brother befriended people through their Jehovah's witnesses meetings that were held in secret in people's homes since Egypt bans such gatherings and attendants could be subject to arrest and imprisonment if discovered.

The couple that hosted the Witnesses meetings, Samia and Naseem, were an extremely wealthy and lovely couple. They owned an apartment overlooking the Nile and another "vacation chalet" only steps from the pyramids. They invited us to their chalet house for barbeques every weekend where their backyard overlooked the three pyramids on the Geezah Plateau at the outskirts of Cairo. Samia and Naseem owned a large vicious and psychotic German Sheppard named

Bruno. He was extremely possessive of the couple and attacked anyone who would even dare to glance their way. He had bitten several of their guests, and at one time landed the electric meter reader in the hospital for a week. He was so out of control that the couple had to build a metal gate, floor to ceiling, inside of their apartment to keep Bruno safely separated from the rest of the apartment or any unsuspecting visitors.

The dog terrorized the entire building but Samia loved him and refused to give him away, even though he had bit her on several occasions while dragging her through the apartment.

Everyone was terrified of Bruno even while he sat impatiently behind his metal gate, staring directly at the guests, and any erratic or sudden moves jolted him into a wild frenzy, violently barking and shaking his metal gate, like a deranged inmate trying to get out at any cost.

Egypt is a vast country with ninety percent of its land covered in desert sand. Moving away from the Nile and the populated areas, sand hills and dunes stretched as far as the eye can see into the horizon.

On one of our day trips, my cousins invited my brother and me for a ride to the red sea, to explore lesser-known archeological sites. Five thousand year-old tombs, pyramids and underground tunnels and cities are scattered throughout the country, buried under the sand, waiting to be excavated. We drove through the desert for hours arriving at an oasis with a large fresh water lake and palm trees. I jumped out of the car and ran through the desert followed by my cousins.

The Burning Cedars

At a distant, I could see a sign posted and as we approached, it read "Land mines. Do not enter." Hundreds of unexploded land mines left over from the Egyptian-Israeli war were scattered throughout the desert and we were walking in the middle of it.

We carefully traced our steps back to the car and hurried away from the area. For several minutes, no one said a word then, as if on queue, we all burst out laughing at what we have just done. We later found out that the area was a military zone and had we been spotted, we would've been arrested and jailed.

RAMZY BAROODY

My mother and I touring the ancient Egyptian tombs outside of Cairo.

Uncle Tony (left), me, cousin Rhona and my mom in front of a pyramid in Egypt.

My brother and I at the oasis by the Red Sea.

The Burning Cedars

CHAPTER THIRTY-EIGHT

THE OLD MAN ON THE STREET

My aunt's apartment was a few streets away from ours and I walked there every afternoon to visit with my cousins. One afternoon as I was walking back from her apartment, an older man approached me and began to ask me questions about my background, where I lived and so on.

He said that he knew my dad from school back in Lebanon and he can prove it by showing me pictures of the two of them he had in his apartment. He kept insisting that I should go up to his apartment with him while trying unsuccessfully to speak with a Lebanese dialect and failing miserably.

After a few minutes, I was getting very suspicious of this person and concerned for my safety as I had no doubt that this man's intentions were suspect at best.

I began to plan an exit strategy and just then, I glanced down the street and saw a policeman standing on the corner.

By then, realizing that I had no intention of acquiescing to his demands, the old man's tone shifted to a more belligerent and threatening one.

The Burning Cedars

I knew that it was time for me to take action and just as I was getting ready to yell to the policeman, I looked over and the old man had disappeared as quickly as he had appeared a few minutes earlier.

I was shaken but thankful that he had left and didn't know what to make of this incident, so when I got home, I told my mother all about it and she was enraged and wanted to confront this man. She told me to take her to where he allegedly lived and I took her there.

He had told me that he lived on the sixth floor of the ten-story apartment building where we stood and when we got there, my mom quickly scanned the names of the tenants displayed next to the door buzzer in the lobby. There was no name listed on the sixth floor buzzer indicating the apartment was vacant but my mom rang it anyway but no one answered, so we turned around and went back home, with my mom still furious and I, shaken up and confused.

My mom had always warned us against speaking to or trusting in strangers. Luckily I heeded her advice that day and was able to distinguish truth from fiction. I shudder to think of what would have happened to me had I taken this man on his word and gone up to his apartment with him.

I thought to myself that I managed to live through war, injury and famine only to have this happen to me in a country which was supposed to be our safe haven from all harm.

RAMZY BAROODY

The Burning Cedars

CHAPTER THIRTY-NINE

GOING BACK

Nine months into our stay in Egypt, the war in Lebanon abruptly ends and a truce was drafted between all the fighting factions. The airport once again opened while a "peace keeping" force, comprised of neighboring Arab country soldiers, was dispatched to oversee the peace and ensure all factions abide by the treaty.

Soon after, my dad's employer called him back to work as life was gradually returning to normal and we eagerly prepared for our return.

Our stay in Egypt provided a much-needed respite from all the chaos that was taking place in our country, but, at last, it was time to go home again.

My dad booked the earliest flight available and we said our goodbyes to my cousins, neighbors and friends. To our surprise, on our last day the person who showed the most emotion to our leaving was our housekeeper, who broke down and cried the entire day as we tried to pack and comfort her at the same time.

Had we not known about her food thievery, our farewell to her would have been a more touching and sincere one. My dad said that she was crying because her free meal ticket was about to expire.

Towards the end of the day and with tears in her eyes, our housekeeper took turns hugging all of us goodbye. When she got to my mom, she took her aside to tell her something important. We all thought she was going to confess to taking all that food. Instead, she had a request: "Please send me a coat when you get back to Lebanon." She asked, " I need a warm coat and cannot afford one, please send me a coat."

With mixed emotions, my mom assured her that she will try her best to send a coat, but never did, not out of spite or anger, but rather because my dad never agreed to it.

Till this day, my mom remains upset to not fulfilling her promise and sending that coat in spite of the maids' dishonestly.

The Burning Cedars

CHAPTER FORTY

STARTING OVER

All three of my aunts along with their husbands were waiting for us at the airport upon our return to Beirut. A joyful reunion ensued, after which we split up into three groups to be driven home.

"Where are we going?" I asked my dad.

Our house was unlivable after the explosion in need of major repair. None of my aunts could accommodate us for an extended period of time, and most hotels were still closed or damaged by the war.

Yet my dad had apparently pre-arranged everything from Egypt: "One of my cousins is out of the country and his furnished apartment is available until our house is fixed. I made arrangements for us to stay there," he said.

It was eight in the evening when we left the airport and although the fighting had stopped, it remained unsafe to be out late at night as rogue armed militias roamed the streets at times. We drove up the mountain to our village, passing several army checkpoints and arrived in Aley an hour later. We passed our house on the way, which had been abandoned since we left. From the outside, one could not tell that a mortar shell had exploded inside nine months earlier, destroying a large portion of the house. The garden was overgrown with weeds

The Burning Cedars

and there were no lights anywhere in the building or on the streets. Electricity was in short supply and came on erratically for only several hours a day. Although water supply was also intermittent, we were lucky in Aley to have several natural springs supplying clean drinking water year-round.

My aunts said shops are beginning to open back up and several bakeries had also resumed their services.

Our temporary residence turned out to be just up the street from our house. The apartment was on the top floor of a four-story old stone building, with identical internal and external configuration to our old house as it was modeled after it and built shortly after my grandfather built our house. Luckily however, this apartment had been totally updated and remodeled only a few years earlier. Although only a few blocks away from our house, this building remained intact during the war and was in move-in condition. The apartment was fully furnished and being on the top floor, afforded a magnificent view of the surrounding mountains, Beirut and the Mediterranean Sea.

On the first floor lived my dad's other cousin, Mary, with her husband, the pharmacist who took over my grandfather's Pharmacy after his death. They lived with their two sons, Ramzy, whom I was named after, and Raja. Mary was a kind woman who loved cats and had seven of the most beautiful all white longhaired Persians. She knew I loved cats and would call them all into the kitchen when I visited in the afternoons. She always promised to give me a cat from the new litter but would end up keeping them for herself.

With the exception of a few skirmishes between the different factions, the truce seemed to be holding and my dad started looking for a school where he could enroll us for the upcoming year. Our old school, Beirut Evangelical, had been destroyed in the war so my dad enrolled us in the local high school in Aley, within walking distance from the house. He himself had attended that school when he was young and although it was not as prestigious as Beirut Evangelical, it had a good reputation in the area.

By enrolling us in the Aley school, my dad failed to consider that my brother and I would be the only Christians in the school.

After the war, most Christians had left the town and now Aley and its schools is predominantly Druze. Luckily, neither my brother nor I were hassled by anyone at the school because of our religion.

We both refrained from discussing any political or religious topics with classmates and focused predominantly on our education.

The school had a decent and challenging curriculum and we immersed ourselves in our studies, glad to be back in Lebanon and back in school.

Although the new school offered a fresh start, I felt just as isolated and anti-social as I always had. I was friendly to everyone but befriended no one and again, our hour-long lunch breaks presented an awkward and uncomfortable time for me. The difference this time is that I was able to walk home for lunch which I did daily and was glad to do so. I obtained a special permission card allowing me to leave the premises during the lunch hour and when the noon bell rang, I ran past the gate guard and in fifteen minutes I was home.

The Burning Cedars

In Lebanon most people eat lunch around two pm so my schedule presented a major inconvenience for my grandmother, who usually cooked our meals. Most days she had not even began cooking lunch when I arrived and I had to settle for a sandwich or leftovers. Nevertheless, It gave me great joy and comfort to come home everyday, even to hear my grandmother complaining that she refuses to start cooking this early and if we did not like it, to get ourselves a maid!

A few weeks passed and my dad assembled a crew to fix our house. The place needed major renovations and they estimated a minimum of six months and $30,000 dollars to complete the project. In the meantime, our temporary living quarters were comfortable and we were in no hurry to leave.

Both my dad and uncle were back at work, we were back in school and my mother and grandmother resumed their relationship where they had left off, bickering and arguing daily.

At last everything was almost back to normal.

RAMZY BAROODY

The Burning Cedars

CHAPTER FORTY-ONE

UNIVERSAL COLLEGE OF ALEY

The renovations were finished and we moved back home. The truce was fragile but holding and both my brother and I were doing well in our new school. I missed my old school but enjoyed being able to walk to and from my new one. I took the same route every day, down the long flight of steps at the end of our street, past the old spring water fountain with its source deep inside the mountains, its icy-cold, sweet tasting water was the main water source to our village for hundreds of years prior to indoor plumbing.

I continued through the vegetable market, past the sidewalk display stands of fresh fruits and vegetables, where my grandmother would get into long and heated arguments with the shop keepers trying to convince them to reduce their prices. Down another flight of steps, through narrow alleys weaving back and forth through the steep mountainside leading to the metal gates of our school.

The school was divided into four buildings, with the oldest being the library, which also housed the faculty and administrative offices. Adjacent to it was a newly constructed cafeteria building and a snack shop. The classrooms were in a new four story large building at the bottom of the hill overlooking the surrounding mountains and in the distant you could see Beirut and the Mediterranean Sea. Midway between the classroom building and the library/cafeteria buildings was a large playground where students played soccer and basketball on their lunch hour.

The curriculum was that of a typical high school and included math, science, Arabic, history, geography, physical education and your choice of English or French. English was my favorite subject while Physical Education was my least favorite.

Not only did PE require physical strength and stamina, both of which I lacked, but also involved working in teams and building comradeships, skills that I still lacked and shunned away from.
Although my brother and I attended the same school, I rarely saw or spoke to him during the day. I walked back and forth to school by myself daily, but then again, I was used to my solitary life. This time however, I did not feel lonely and deserted knowing that home was a short walk away.

The school year went by quickly and I was looking forward to the summer vacation. I was devastated when the end-of-year grade reports were distributed and I learned that I flunked math and had to report to summer school. I expected my parents to be angry with me for failing one of my courses, but instead, they were supportive, understanding, and compassionate.

The Burning Cedars

Perhaps because of all the pandemonium we had gone through, the difficulty of adjusting to a new school or the fact that I had never previously failed a class, my parents had nothing but encouraging and comforting words of advice for me. My dad even hired a chauffeur to drive me back and forth to summer school: "It's bad enough that you have to go to summer school, I don't want you to walk there everyday," he insisted.

I had to attend school three days a week plus Saturdays from eight am till noon. There were close to a half dozen other kids in summer class with me and we spent our days in the library going over our daily math assignments, then we were to be tested on the material at the end of the six weeks.

It was Saturday morning, four weeks into our summer class when everything came to an abrupt halt. I was neither able to complete summer school nor go back to that school ever again after that day.

RAMZY BAROODY

The Burning Cedars

CHAPTER FORTY-TWO

FAMILIAR SIGHTS AND SOUNDS

Saturday morning in August was a beautiful summer day but I had to get ready to be picked up to go to my morning class. I was very unhappy about having to spend my days cooped up in an old library studying. What made this worse was that the west-facing wall of the library, with its floor to ceiling windows overlooked Beirut and the Mediterranean Sea where I would have rather been spending my Saturday, swimming and soaking up the sun. I sat by these windows for hours daydreaming about all the lucky kids enjoying their vacations, sunbathing on the warm sands and swimming in the deep blue waters of the Mediterranean. I could see the white foam from the waves as they crashed against the towering rocks rising from the sea, and in the distant, all the ships sailing in and out of the port, loading and unloading their cargo. The sun reflected so brightly off the waters that if you stared at it long enough, you saw dark spots in front of your eyes for several minutes after looking away.

RAMZY BAROODY

Aley was situated high up in the mountains and during the day, the sea breeze, heated by the sun, funneled through and up the mountain, washing over our village on it way to higher elevations.

Some days you could almost smell that distinctive Mediterranean salt-water aroma as it traveled on the warm gentle breezes, passing through the pine forests on the mountain slopes.

Once they reached our village, the sea breezes cooled and condensed into wispy clouds that by late afternoon thicken into a layer of fog blanketing the mountains and obscuring our view of Beirut and beyond.

On that August morning, I was in my usual seat in the library by the window going over my assignments and periodically glancing out the window at Beirut. As I looked out, I saw a flash of light in the center of the city, followed by a muffled boom and a column of smoke, followed by another and another. All the kids ran to the windows looking out as several more columns of smoke billowed out into the sky. One of the teachers ran in and told us to go home, but no one knew exactly what was going on. I gathered my books and quickly walked home. Both my dad and uncle were still at work in Beirut and we turned on the radio and listened intently. Fighting had broken out between the Syrian "peace keeping" force and the Christian militias. The Syrian army, which was initially deployed to oversee the truce, had aligned itself with the Muslim militias fighting against the Christians who opposed their presence in the country.

At hearing the news, my mom became hysterical, concerned about my dad who worked close to where the fighting was taking place.

The Burning Cedars

Unable to reach my dad or my uncle by phone, all we could do is wait and pray that they are able to escape safely. The flashes of light and the booming sounds were intensifying and still no sign of my dad or uncle. Several hours went by and we saw my uncle's Austin pull up followed by my dad's skylark. We all took a long sigh of relief but now, we were again in the middle of another war.

RAMZY BAROODY

From my school in Aley, I had a clear view of Beirut in the distant and the unmistakable sights and sounds of the re-initiation of the fighting between the Christian East and Muslim West Beirut.

The Burning Cedars

CHAPTER FORTY-THREE

ON THE RUN AGAIN

Since the Syrian army occupied most of Lebanon, the Christian militias were surrounded on three fronts in east Beirut and the surrounding hills with their back to the sea.

"We will defeat then push the Christians into the sea" announced one Muslim militia leader. The Christians, outnumbered and outgunned, were faced with a fight or die scenario, and they decided to fight for their lives.

Once again, we were living a nightmare, which did not seem to want to end. Gradually the fighting intensified and spread throughout the country like wildfire. All we could do is hunker down in our recently renovated house, blaming ourselves for returning to Lebanon so hastily. The daily bombardment resumed but now, the Syrian army was using new and more powerful weapons. Multi-rocket launchers were positioned only a few yards from our house and the response came swiftly and violently from Beirut. The airport closed once again and we were stranded.

This time, however, we decided that we were not going to be sitting ducks, in wait for another mortar to blow up our house with us in it.

The Burning Cedars

The very next day, we packed our suitcases and waited for a break in the fighting to make our way up the mountain to the relative safety of the Bekaa valley in the northern part of the country by the Syrian border. "What shall I do with my parakeets?" I asked my dad.

Several months prior, my uncle had surprised me with two beautiful green and yellow parakeets, knowing how much I liked them. Now I faced a dilemma, unable to leave the birds behind, unwilling to set them loose and unsure if we would be able to check into a hotel with the birds. I decided to bring them along.

Around one in the afternoon that day, the fighting had stopped and we started on our way north to the Bekaa valley.

The Syrian army was in full control of the valley and its remote location and the encircling mountains shielded it from any mortar shells from Beirut. The trip was long and perilous as we drove through many villages under the control of rogue militias, poised to fight, abduct or kill anyone they deemed sympathetic to the other side.
We drove through multiple checkpoints manned by armed militiamen of various affiliations and factions including Syrian, Palestinian and Lebanese Muslim and Druze.

Several hours into our trip we reached the summit at 30,000 feet. From here, you could see the entire Bekaa valley all the way to the Syrian border. It was now a steep downhill drive zigzagging through the mountainside. Most cars and trucks we passed on the road belonged to the Syrian army or their armed supporters.

Tanks and truck-mounted rocket launchers whizzed by at great speeds on their way to battle. It was an eerie and unsettling sight knowing that an untold number of casualties will fall to this entire military might and no one can do anything to stop it.

Another hour in the car and we were finally in the valley. On our way to the hotel, we passed by some railroad tracks and an old abandoned train. With tears in his eyes, my uncle turned to me saying: "This is the old train which transported people and goods from Aley to Zahle. Do you remember us walking to the station in the afternoon to watch this train as it disappeared into the tunnel with steam billowing out of its chimney?"

"Yes" I replied sadly, knowing that those days are gone forever.

The Burning Cedars

CHAPTER FORTY-FOUR

THE BEKAA VALEY

*W*e arrived at the hotel around 4:30 that afternoon and after checking in, headed to the dining hall for dinner. I was concerned that the front desk may not allow me to keep my parakeet cage in the room, but they could not care less. The only complaints we got was from the housekeeper who was fed up with vacuuming the spilled bird seeds out of the shag bedroom carpet, so I spread some newspapers under the cage to catch the seeds and that made her stop complaining about "the damn mess these birds are making."

Our hotel was a converted old mansion with intriquately carved stonewalls, spacious hallways leading to large and sunny rooms, giving the place a homey feel where we felt comfortable and safe. To get to the hotel you had to go off the main road, through a large old iron gate leading to immaculately kept gardens surrounding the beautiful hotel. Behind the hotel was a large swimming pool and tennis courts.

The place felt like a calm and serene oasis where death and destruction was somehow kept at bay outside those imposing gates. In reality, chaos and desolation prevailed everywhere and armed soldiers with their tanks and rocket launchers killed indiscriminately.

The Burning Cedars

On most days we stayed on the hotel grounds and ventured out to the market only briefly to buy food or bird seeds! Although there was not much to do during the day other than listening to the news or reading the newspapers, I was glad to be out of harm's way for the time being.

Several weeks went by and the fighting abruptly stopped. As with previous cessations of the fighting, no resolution or compromises were made by any of the fighting factions but as my dad would call it "Time to re-stock on weapons cease fires," and unfortunately, he was right.

Nevertheless, when the fighting stopped we decided to go back home and on Sunday morning, we checked out and drove back, not knowing what to expect when we got home. Luckily, this time the house had been spared, so we settled in and waited for what was to come next.

RAMZY BAROODY

The Burning Cedars

CHAPTER FORTY-FIVE

MY PARAKEETS PREFERRED FREEDOM TO THEIR METAL CAGE!

*I*t was the beginning of October and schools were still closed. Food supplies trickled in and with the exception of a few small stores, most of the market shops were closed and boarded up. Cease-fires were implemented then broken daily and the heaviest fighting took place at night, coming to a tense halt during the day with many infractions in between.

To alleviate my boredom, I began planting corn seeds in our front yard and was very proud of my six plants that sprouted several weeks later. I methodically tended to my corn, watering them daily and watching them grow into full mature plants. After a few months I was able to pick three cornhusks from one of my plants and shared my bounty with the family. My brother bought a few chickens, which he tended to constantly. Some days I helped my brother clean after his chickens and the few pigeons he was also raising.

Yet my parakeets continued to be my pride and joy and I sat by their cage for hours watching them as they delicately and lovingly groomed themselves and each other. Some days I let them out of their cage and watched them fly around the room until they tire themselves out, land on the floor then wobble back to their cage. One day I let them out of their cage not realizing that the hallway window was open. They immediately headed for it, flying out into the yard. I grabbed their cage and ran after them, chasing them around from one tree to the next, hoping that seeing their little metal prison would entice them to willingly get back in it. Instead, the sight of the cage repelled them even further away until they eventually disappeared into the forest, and that was the last I saw of my beloved parakeets.

Gradually the war intensified and streets were swarming with Syrian soldiers and their tanks. The shelling was unrelenting and once again we were faced with the dilemma to stay or leave. One night the shelling turned so violent that my dad swore he would take us away the very next morning. By dawn, we packed our car and headed back to the Bekaa valley, again. Once there, we stopped at the same hotel we had previously stayed in but they were full to capacity with no rooms available.

A few miles down the road, we found another hotel with rooms available. This one was on the main road and with much less charm and appeal than the first. The first floor was an open-air restaurant with steps at the far end leading to the rooms on the second floor. The restaurant was packed with Syrian soldiers eating, drinking and just hanging out, and we soon discovered why this place was so overflowing with soldiers.

The Burning Cedars

CHAPTER FORTY-SIX

SOLDIERS, TANKS AND GUNS

We checked into our rooms and after unpacking, my mom and I walked outside to the upper deck to enjoy the view and the nice weather. We walked to the edge of the deck which overlooked the fertile fields of the Bekaa valley hoping to see farmers tilling the soil and planting their crops. "I wonder if we're allowed to go down there and pick some fruit," I naively asked my mom.

We peaked over the deck wall and were shocked by what we saw. Instead of farmers planting and harvesting, the valley was teeming with thousands of tents, trucks and tanks, as far as the eye could see. Dingy brown and green-colored equipment and camouflaged tents littered the place. Directly underneath the hotel, Syrian army men were washing their clothes in plastic bins while others were hanging them out to dry in the sun. Others were meticulously polishing and cleaning their guns while cannons were being loaded up with large shells in preparation for what looked like an imminent assault. It was a depressing and terrifying sight.

The Burning Cedars

I never understood why people are filled with such malevolence and hatred for one another. We senselessly kill and destroy in the name of religion, which by nature is meant to bring us closer together and teach us to respect life and seek atonement and purity. We strive to be more God-like, yet accomplish everything He despises the most.

When we realized that we were in the middle of a Syrian army base, we became very uneasy staying at this hotel so my dad and uncle drove around looking for other hotels in the area, but none had rooms available.

Like us, many families from Beirut and other hard hit areas have traveled here to escape the war. Everyone was on edge, uncertain of the future of our country.

That night I had difficulty sleeping so I walked outside, staring endlessly at the sky and the majestic snow-capped mountains. The high elevation and lack of air pollution combined to form an exquisite canvas of the most beautiful night sky, with stars that shimmered so brightly you could almost reach out and grab them. The merciful moon still extended his silver rays over undeserving evil men and the brisk cold wind washed over us, as if gently nudging us to come together and put aside our hatreds and dislikes for one another.

This calm and natural beauty however, fell on blind eyes and deaf ears that only saw death and heard painful cries.

It was the end of summer and the nights were getting colder. Against this beautiful backdrop, an ugly scene was unfolding in the valley below. Thousands of men loaded their guns and hauled their big cannons into position. Their metal tanks violently plowing the soil where crops of corn and wheat once grew.

We suspected an assault was being planned, yet what unfolded shattered what little hope remained of a peaceful resolution to this senseless war.

The Burning Cedars

CHAPTER FORTY-SEVEN

THIS DAY WAS A TURNING POINT IN OUR LIVES

Three days after arriving at the hotel in the Bekaa valley in the north of Lebanon for the second time, things looked gloomier than ever. Throughout our time here and in spite of our distant location, we could hear sounds of explosions and gunfire on the other side of the mountain particularly at night.

Sunday afternoon at four, we were relaxing in our rooms when a powerful explosion shook the hotel, rattling windows, doors and what was left of our nerves. Shortly after, another explosion, then another in methodical succession.

We jumped out of our beds and looked out the window but saw nothing. The smell of gunpowder filled the room and we suspected that we were under attack. Several minutes went by and a new barrage of explosions, so we hurried down to the ground floor where the restaurant was located. The place was swarming with Syrian soldiers who seemed unconcerned with what was taking place outside.

We stood in the middle of the dining hall bewildered and terrified. A Syrian soldier ran towards me with a look of pain and anguish: "Where's the bathroom?" he asked.

The Burning Cedars

I didn't answer him, so he urgently asked again: "I need to go to the bathroom, where's the bathroom?" I pointed to the door in the back and he took of in that direction. "What is going on?" I asked my dad. "I don't know but I'm going to find out," he replied. As we huddled in the middle of the restaurant, my dad walked away to make some inquiries, "Don't go outside," my mom yelled and my dad just signaled ok with his hand. Several minutes later, he returned with a distressed look on his face.

"The Syrian army just installed a new long range cannon in the valley capable of shelling East Beirut. East Beirut is the Christian enclave and it was under a major assault, taking heavy artillery fire on many fronts.

Throughout the war and with everything we had gone through, my dad has been the strong and optimistic one. He remained hopeful that the war will end and we could resume a normal life. On that day in the hotel, there was a new glare in his eyes, that of anger, despair and hopelessness. His expressions suggested disgust and fear, faced with the inescapable reality that our future, our very existence, was closely connected to that of our country and we have both arrived at the end of the road, with no prospect of turning back.

There remained no future for us in Lebanon and we were all exhausted by this kind of existence. We had to face reality, take control of our lives by securing a better future for ourselves. That day was a turning point in our lives.

RAMZY BAROODY

"This is it," my dad shouted, "This is the last straw. We are wasting our lives living like this. The kids are missing out on their education, our funds are dwindling, our lives are in constant danger and there's nothing left for us here but death. I am selling the building and we are leaving the country permanently."

The Burning Cedars

CHAPTER FORTY-EIGHT

WE MUST SELL THE BUILDING

*T*he very next morning we packed our bags, checked out of the hotel and drove home. The two hour ride took four hours as many roads were closed and barricaded, rockets were exploding all around us and armed personnel were everywhere. We arrived home around two pm that day and another surprise was awaiting us. The Syrian army had occupied our building, taking over the entire second floor directly above us. Over a dozen army trucks were posted all around our house and soldiers were walking in and out at all hours of the day and night. Across from our front door, a 24-hour watchman had been stationed while armored jeeps and trucks drove by constantly. Our house was a prime location for such a deployment since it faced the town hall, which was also under Syrian army control. The Syrian presence provided us with little sense of security for two main reasons.

First, since entering our country under the pretense of a "peace keeping force," the Syrian army had aligned itself with the Islamic and Palestinian militias, killing, torturing and kidnapping anyone who stood in their way, including men, women and children.

The Burning Cedars

Second, their presence in our building placed us in a dangerous situation, as we are now a prime target of shelling from Christian East Beirut.

We decided that the best way to handle this situation is to totally ignore them while maintaining a low profile, never engaging them in any conversation no matter how trivial. Therefore, we never spoke to nor acknowledged the soldiers while remaining cordial and cautious. Luckily, they were the same with us.

During all this, my dad had been planning and preparing for us to permanently leave the country. Since we had relatives in the US, our first choice was to emigrate there. But the American embassy in Beirut had been closed for some time, so we applied for an immigration visa to Canada instead.

To our surprise, a few weeks later, the Canadian embassy approved our request. At that time thousands of Lebanese Christians were given the green light to emigrate to Canada, an undertaking which was later halted by request of the Lebanese government in an attempt to limit the mass exodus of Christians from the country.

Initially, we were thrilled by the news, yet after careful consideration, my dad decided not to pursue the Canadian offer: "We don't know anyone there," said my dad, "It's very cold, jobs are hard to find and taxes are high."
"Who cares," I replied, "At least we can get out of here."
"I will get you out" my dad promised, "But it will not be to Canada."

Second choice on our list was Paris, France. At one time, Lebanon was a French colony and many Lebanese spoke French and felt a certain connection and camaraderie with the French.

The problem with going to France was that none of us spoke French, with the exception of my dad who could get by with a light conversation. We researched the schools in France and found an American school just outside of Paris where we could continue our education. We were all excited about going to Paris, so much so that I obtained and filled out the school application and began to teach myself French. I was very much looking forward to living in Paris, daydreaming about what our lives would be like strolling down the *Shanzelize*, buying French souvenirs, and taking my mom on a shopping spree at the French boutiques. I bought a postcard of the *Eifel* tower and hung it on the wall by my bed. I imagined what it would be like going up the elevator to the top and looking over the most beautiful city in the world.

All this daydreaming however, could not come to fruition until my dad sells the building. Yet who would be willing or able to invest any money in a building occupied by Syrian soldiers during a civil war?

My dad approached one of our tenants, a well to do shoe storeowner in our village with the offer to buy the building for cash. The man, of the Druze religion, was a shrude businessperson and quick to realize the potential of this offer. He was also aware of our dilemma, being the only Christian family left in town, and that we were eager to sell. All the chips were stacked in his favor and he had the cash to move on this deal quickly.

The Burning Cedars

After several weeks of negotiations, they reached a middle ground on the sale price. Now my dad was having second thoughts on selling the building and remained reluctant to move ahead with the sale of a home which his father built and where he grew up. Many fond memories were attached to this house and his decision to leave it behind was not an easy one.

The assault of from Beirut was escalating in intensity and frequency as we huddled in the dining room night after night trying to get some sleep yet unable to do so.

On one particularly intense night, we heard a loud explosion as the whole building shook. We knew that we were hit but unable to investigate until the following morning. We sat up motionless in our beds all night listening to the horrid sounds of shelling and gunfire outside.

The next morning the fighting died down and we carefully ventured out to inspect the building. A rocket had hit the top floor apartment reducing it to a pile of rubble. The explosion was so powerful that blocks of cement, along with metal piping and wires littered our backyard. Within the hour, my dad was in our tenants' apartment signing the sales agreement for the settled upon sum of $350,000 liras, or $150,000 dollars, in cash.

RAMZY BAROODY

The Burning Cedars

CHAPTER FORTY-NINE

DECIDING ON THE ULTIMATE DESTINATION

At last the building was sold and now we were faced with the overwhelming task of packing what we needed and disposing of or selling what remained. The house was jam packed with "stuff" accumulated throughout the years and anything we could not pack into our suitcases had to be sold or given away. When my grandfather was alive, he accumulated many large pieces of ivory from Africa along with rare carved-wooden statues made from a unique African tree of dark and light wood. We also had paintings from France, entire sets of pure silver tableware along with beautiful Persian rugs from Iran.

My absolute favorite item in the house was a five-foot long ivory tusk, intricately carved and mounted with ivory-carved elephants spanning the entire length of the tusk. The elephants increased in size from one end to the other and when a few of them came loose, I used them as toys, playing with them around the house, unaware of their value or rarity. I loved this piece because it had been placed on top of our piano in the living room for as long as I could remember and during my piano lessons, it somehow inspired me to continue playing late into the night. I would imagine how this tusk came about, the people in Africa sitting on the ground painstakingly and with such mastery carving and transforming this object into a piece of art. Two other pieces of ivory we had were carved to resemble large snails. They were used as candleholders.

In my grandmother's closet she hid a complete set of silverware with carved ivory handles she received as a gift on her wedding day. She also received an ivory necklace and matching earrings carved like a church stained glass, with images of trees, leaves and saints.

My dad's uncle, Samuel, was a world traveler who collected beautiful and rare items from around the globe, many ending up in our house. After one of his many African trips, he gave my grandmother two wooden statues, two feet in height each, carved in the shape of an African warrior's head and neck, complete with all the jewelry worn in battle along with two others shaped like a hippopotamus. They were carved from wood which was almost black in color, and uncle Samuel said they were extremely rare and valuable and their wood used for native medicinal purposes.

My grandmother, who suffered from arthritis, used the hippo statues to support her lower back when she sat down or slept. She said they somehow offered her relief from her back pain. Other carved wooden items he brought back were made of two or three-tone-colored wood, nothing like I have seen before or since.

During our packing frenzy, my dad purchased a large trunk where he packed as many valuable items as he could, including the

The Burning Cedars

ivory and wooden statues, silverware, old dinnerware and two small Persian rugs.

Through brief lulls in the fighting, the airport was partially opened with very limited flights out of the country, mostly to neighboring Arab countries. My dad's plan was for us to return to Egypt, obtain our US visas then continue on from there. My aunt Grace and cousins were still living there so going back to Egypt was the most logical and practical choice under the circumstances. Next we had to decide what to do with all the large items left behind in the house.

My dad wanted to try and sell as much of it as possible and informed everyone of this. Several days prior to our departure, I pulled out an atlas I had for school and began planning where to settle in the US once we got there.

We had relatives in Philadelphia and South Carolina, friends in Dallas, Texas, and we heard that California's weather and scenery resembled that of Lebanon. My dad had visited Florence, South Carolina a few years earlier and said it was a very small town with one main road passing through it. It had one shopping center, several gas stations and churches but nothing else.

Dallas, Texas had two things going for it at that time. The city was booming as a result of the oil revenue, and the TV show Dallas was the number one hit show in Lebanon, portraying Texas living as lavish and extravagant. My dad quickly discounted moving to Dallas explaining that it would be difficult for him to find work in his field there. We heard many good things about California but none of us were genuinely interested in moving there.

My dad said it was too far, "All the way on the other coast," as he put it. My mom was fearful of the earthquakes, and my grandmother objected on the grounds that it was too far from her sister in South Carolina. My brother was the only person eager to move to California: "They have mountains with snow, a beach and mild climate, what else could we ask for?" he insisted. Ultimately we all agreed, with the exception of my brother, that California was off the list as well, leaving us with only one final destination choice, Philadelphia.

Once we decided on where we would settle, I immediately started researching the Philadelphia area. According to my "obviously inaccurate" references, Philadelphia enjoyed temperate climate with cool winters and sunny pleasant summers. The area receives a marginal amount of snow in the winter and is seen as the gateway between NY and Washington, making it a desirable and bustling metropolis. As a snow lover, I was excited to move to Philadelphia. My dad liked the idea of being close to NY City, where he planned to revive his import/export business.

But most importantly, we had family living there, transplants of the South Carolina Baroody's, and although they are second and third generation Lebanese, we felt that their guidance and support in a foreign country would be an invaluable asset.

The Burning Cedars

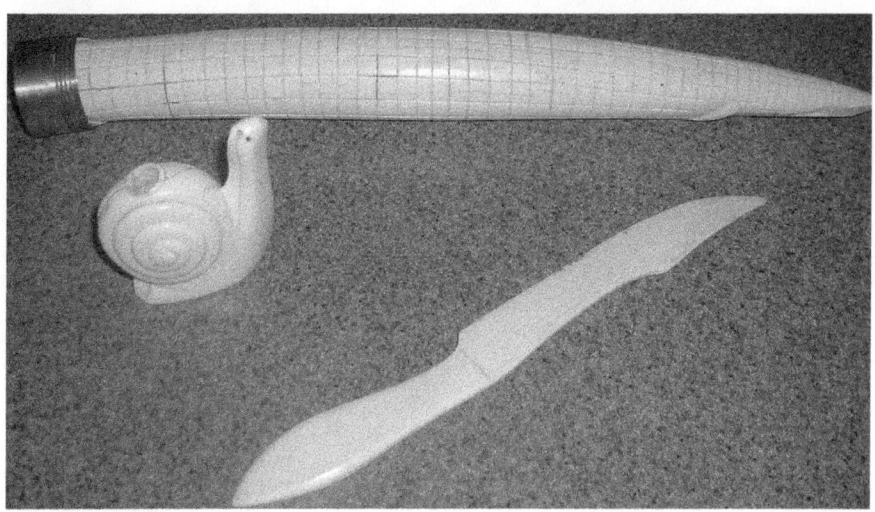

My dad's uncle Samuel traveled the world collecting rare and valuable items, many of which he gave to us, like rare wooden carved statues and beautiful ivory from Africa.

RAMZY BAROODY

The Burning Cedars

CHAPTER FIFTY

THE ESTATE SALE DEBACLE

Our last week in Lebanon went by so quickly, we all felt we needed more time to organize and pack. The plane reservations had been made and my dad called my aunt in Cairo to inform her the date of our arrival.

Unlike our previous trip in Cairo, however, this time we decided that we would stay in a hotel until we can rent an apartment. To cut down on expenses, my dad asked my aunt to reserve rooms for us in the "least expensive" hotel in Cairo she could find. We announced to everyone that on Thursday of that week we were having an estate sale. As was customary with my dad, he was having second thoughts selling all the antique furniture and valuables in the house. Items that he grew up with, filled with fond memories of his childhood and of his father who died when he was very young, never having the chance to get to know him growing up. He considered packing everything into a storage container and shipping it to his aunt in South Carolina, but to do so was cost prohibitive and none of us wanted to keep this "old outdated broken down stuff" which today would have been designated as valuable antiques. We were also unsure of the length of time we would be staying in Egypt or if we would even be able to continue to the US from there.

Thursday came and I woke up early in a morning with mixed emotions about what we were embarking upon. Starting a new life somewhere else would not be easy and leaving my home, along with all the memories attached to every square inch of it made me very sad. I am not the kind of person to get attached to material possessions but everything in that house had a history and a story attached to it.

My grandfather worked day and night to build and furnish this house, and although it was old and drafty, we were the envy of many friends and family who were overwhelmed by the "vastness" and "sophistication" of the estate. Whenever she came over, grandma Souad, my mother's mother, constantly complained that one needed a bicycle to get from one end of the house to the other.

Around seven am that Thursday, people started lining up for our estate sale. Many who showed up I did not recognize including alleged friends and relatives, eager for a bargain. By noon, the sale turned into total mayhem, with people hauling anything they could carry and just walking out with it. Apparently, some relatives felt that they were entitled to whatever was in the house, insulted by the fact they had to pay for it.

"You can't take it with you and you can't leave it here," they argued, "so it really holds no value for you. Why can't we just have it for nothing?" and most of them did. Others used the "we're poor and have no money" technique, while still others made it like

The Burning Cedars

they were doing us a favor taking this "junk" out of the house.

When all was said and done, the house was empty and we hardly made enough money to pay for the cab fare to the airport. By the end of that day, we all had that "deer caught in headlights" look, shocked and bewildered by what had taken place and the abhorrence of human nature. Our own family was reduced to vultures encircling a wounded prey, nipping and tucking at it from all sides until nothing is left but the dry brittle bones of the carcass. We were all deeply hurt by the shameless behavior of people who called themselves our friends and our family, all of whom saw this as an opportunity to grab and run, rather than console and comfort.

RAMZY BAROODY

The Burning Cedars

CHAPTER FIFTY-ONE

FAREWELL

Thursday night we arranged our suitcases neatly by the front door and went to bed. I was too excited and nervous to sleep so I sat up in bed most of the night planning and visualizing what it would be like to live in the US.

It was an unusually quiet night with only sporadic fire faintly heard from Beirut and I hoped this continued till the next day. As soon as daylight broke, I was out of bed, walking throughout our empty house with a profound sadness for having to leave.

As I walked outside to the backyard, my black and white cat was waiting for me on the steps looking for food, zigzagging back and forth between my legs and meowing incessantly. "I'm sorry I have to leave you," I said in a low voice with tears running down my cheeks, "I will miss you most of all." She just looked at me, undaunted by my emotions, and then I reached over and petted her on the head. She turned around and made her way down the garden path, disappearing into the bushes. It was the last time I would see my beloved cat.

I hoped she finds a new home with people to love and care for her as much as I did, and I sat on the steps crying for over an hour until my uncle found me and with comforting words, assured me that she will be ok.

Three pm came and our taxi picked us up and we headed for the airport. We made it there on time and boarded our plane. I argued with my brother about who gets the window seat, then my mom offered me hers, saying she does not want to look out the window anyway. "Will I ever be back?" I thought to myself, "What's going to happen to us?" The plane sped up and began its ascend while I looked out the window at the beautiful mountains, the green pastures and the blue Mediterranean Sea.

From up here, everything on the ground looked serene and peaceful.

From up here, there was no war and no killing, no hatred or bloodshed. Only beauty and tranquility.

From up here, I'm the shy and lonely kid hiding under the olive trees waiting for my school bell to ring.

From up here, my brother and I were as estranged as ever yet happy and content.

From up here, my mother and grandmother fought endlessly yet at days end, neither harbored malice or ill will for the other.

From up here, my dad was as frugal as ever, yet kind and loving, scolding my teachers for threatening to spank me with a wooden ruler had I missed my homework or done poorly on an exam.

But most of all, from up here, my kind and loving uncle was by my side as always and this gave me joy and comfort, knowing that everything will be ok as long as he is with me.

The Burning Cedars

The plane climbed higher and clouds obscured my view of everything. It was a somber two-hour flight into the unknown.

RAMZY BAROODY

My brother in our backyard on our last day prior to leaving bidding farewell to our cat and his prized pigeons.

The Burning Cedars

CHAPTER FIFTY TWO

HOTEL "NITTO KRIS"

Our plane landed in Cairo at seven thirty in the evening and after collecting our baggage, we headed outside looking for my aunt or her husband to pick us up. Instead, cousin Rhona's father-in-law, Loutfy, was waiting for us. My aunt sent him in her place with instructions to take us directly to the hotel.

We drove through the heavily congested streets of Cairo, eventually pulling up to an old dilapidated building in the heart of downtown Cairo. "What is this?" my mom inquired. "This is the hotel," Loutfy answered, "your husband told us to look for the cheapest hotel we could find, and this is it."

At first we thought this was a bad joke and waited for Loutfy to break out in laughter yelling "got ya!," but he didn't. He stepped out of the car and began hastily unloading our baggage as we defiantly remained inside, refusing to get out.

Loutfy looked annoyed by our objections to stay at this hotel and said that it was late and he was not about to drive around all night looking for another hotel. Besides, this is what my dad asked for. My dad, who had been quite throughout all this suddenly spoke: "We are here now so let's check in."

The Burning Cedars

The name of the hotel was "Nitto Kris" which, I assume, means something in the ancient Egyptian language since it made no sense in Arabic. The interior of the hotel looked even worse than its exterior. It was a four-story rectangular building with a central open-air court. The steps leading to the rooms were metal and looked like fire escape ladders.

Down below in the middle court, dozens of people were walking around, eating, bathing and doing their laundry. Remnants of paint were peeling off the walls and water was dripping from several cracks in the ceilings.

The first thing you see when you walk into the room is the old, dust covered broken down furniture scattered halfhazerdly throughout. The beds were rusted pieces of metal with a mismatched, filthy, stained (some with blood stains) mattresses covered in equally dirty, ripped and stained sheets. There was one bathroom *per floor* at the far end of the hallway which, needless to say, none of us dared to venture into. Although they were all thinking it, my uncle finally had to say it: "This is a brothel." "What's a brothel?" I asked. My mom then quickly answered, "Don't worry about it, we're getting out of here." By then it was close to ten o'clock at night and we had no idea where to go from here.

I could see my mom getting gradually more hysterical with every passing minute and she refused to sit down or touch anything. Her germ phobia was kicking into high gear and she paced frantically around the room, almost on tip toe, clutching her bag with both arms close to her chest, refusing to put it down anywhere. My mom's heightened sense of repugnance and disgust was contagious as we had been on our feet the entire time as well. My mom shrieked and convulsed in terror if we even dared to as much as lean against anything in the room.

Several more hours went by and my dad maintained that we needed to stay here for at least that night, promising to move us to another hotel the following day. Seeing that my dad was refusing to leave, my mom went downstairs to the corner store and bought a box of large trash bags, a pair of scissors and gloves.

Like a mad person on a wild mission, she tore through the bags, cutting them open and laying them all over everything in the room. When she was finished, the room looked like a quarantined operating area covered in shiny black plastic. Even the door knobs were sealed with plastic cover along with everything that we might touch, brush against or even look at! By three am, my mom was finished quarantining the room and we were allowed to sit down on our assigned trash bags.

Fully clothed, we tried to get some sleep but my mom kept waking us up with her bag ripping noises pursuing her quest to cover every exposed square inch of the room with plastic bags.

I managed to doze off for several hours then woke up around six in the morning to find my mom standing in the doorway holding her bag: "Where are you going?" I asked. "Your dad and I are going to find a rental apartment we can move into" she said as she was pulling him half-asleep out the door. I thought my mother had this time finally gone off the deep end.

The Burning Cedars

In a city of over ten million people, the scarcity of apartments was dire and finding a descent one at such short notice was almost impossible. We locked ourselves in the room and waited for my parents to return.

Several hours later they came back and with a big smile on their faces, announced that they had rented a furnished apartment in the Zamalek area, the same upscale neighborhood we had lived in previously, and this apartment was even closer to my aunt's house than our previous one.

Before finishing their announcement, we were out the door and on the street hailing a taxi to our new home.

RAMZY BAROODY

The Burning Cedars

CHAPTER FIFTY-THREE

WAITING FOR THE CALL FROM THE AMERICAN EMBASSY

*O*ur apartment was a very nice fully furnished two bedroom, one bath on the second floor of a newly constructed building overlooking a quiet side street in the heart of the ritzy Zamalek neighborhood. The only drawback was the mosque across the street where five times a day beginning at five am, loud prayers were broadcast over the speakerphone calling Muslim worshipers to prayers and waking up everyone else. We eventually got used to the prayers and enjoyed our new place tremendously. Around the corner from the mosque was a shopping center with dress shops, a dry cleaner and my favorite, the British hamburger chain restaurant, Wimpy's.

Aside from their famous burgers, Wimpy's served the most decadent and delicious ice cream Sundays, and my favorite was called *Yasmine*. It was served in a humongous glass bowl overflowing with six scoops of your choice of ice cream with chocolate and caramel syrup, topped with fresh fruit and whipped cream.

RAMZY BAROODY

Yasmine was heaven on the taste buds, and hell on the waistline. I must've gained ten pounds the first month we were there so I limited my heavenly indulgence to one night per week. Wimpy's was much more than a fast food chain, it was a social gathering place where friends and family met, ate and listened to a mix of Arabic, British and French music.

My aunt's house was one side street away from Wimpy's and there's where we met our cousins almost nightly, spending hours talking, eating and just hanging out.

Throughout all this food and fun, we did not lose sight of our main objective in coming to Egypt, and that is to obtain our immigration papers to the US. Within a week of our arrival, we submitted all the necessary paperwork to the American embassy and awaited their response. They never give you an exact timeframe as to when a decision will be rendered so all we could do is wait and hope for the best. Six months into our stay in Egypt and we heard nothing from the American Embassy. My dad remained positive but with a backup plan of emigrating to France in the event we were not accepted to the US. We researched living in France and my dad looked into the International school for English speakers just outside of Paris where my brother and I could continue our education. My dad had been to Paris on several business trips and was familiar with the city, its shops, restaurants and schools. His favorite Parisian restaurant was *The Hippo* and he promised to take us there as soon as we arrive. I was actually very excited about the possibility of living in Paris and learning French and spent many hours daydreaming about what life would be like for us there.

The Burning Cedars

First thing I would do is call all my cousins: "I live in Paris now and you can come and visit whenever you want," and I would say this in French. Beirut is only a four-hour plane ride to Paris and the French and the Lebanese have a long history together.

At one time, Lebanon was a French colony and most Lebanese speak both French and Arabic. I was one of the few in my family to attend a British school and to never learn French. Most private schools in Lebanon were run by catholic nuns who spoke and taught only in French. When the sixth month came to an end and we still heard nothing from the US embassy, I was almost certain that we would end up living in France and planned everything accordingly. One day out of the blue, we got a phone call from the American Embassy to schedule an interview appointment with the counselor. We were all thrilled by the news with the exception of my uncle.

RAMZY BAROODY

The Burning Cedars

CHAPTER FIFTY-FOUR

HEARTBREAK FOR UNCLE TONY

At the time, I was still a minor and did not have to go to the embassy with my parents. Their appointment was at two pm that afternoon but my parents were too excited to wait and they left the house early that morning. We stayed in the apartment watching the clock on the day that seemed endless. My cousins called periodically to check in but we had no news for them. By four pm we still had not heard anything and we were all on edge. Every time the phone rang, we all jumped up but it was my cousins again. Around four, my parents pulled up in a taxi and my mom walked into the house first: "Ta dah" she joyfully announced holding up her passport to the page where an official looking red white and blue stamp was marked. No more needed to be said and we started jumping up and down. My dad walked in next looking more relieved than I have seen him in a long time: "They approved us for a six month open visitor visa," he announced. An open visa means that it can be renewed multiple times, but this was not the permanent residency we were hoping for.

Nevertheless, my dad said that once we get into the US, we will hire an attorney and they can start working on our residency papers. We were all jumping up and down of joy with the exception of my uncle: "What are you so happy about," my uncle angrily interrupted, "They never called me in for an interview, so what's going to happen to me now. I will have to go back to Beirut. I won't be able to come with you." My uncle's anger quickly turned into despondency and he ran into his room weeping uncontrollably.

Our happiness turned into apprehension and disappointment over my uncle's unfortunate situation. My dad ran after him trying to console him by saying that he may still hear from them at anytime. Since we all applied for our visas at the same time, we were genuinely concerned as to why my uncle was never called in for an interview. My dad methodically rationalized the situation and concluded that it was probably because my uncle was unmarried and with no immediate family left behind in Lebanon. This was negatively viewed by the embassy, as he was unlikely to leave the US and return home once his visa expires. We also heard that the Lebanese government had asked both the American and Canadian embassies to limit issuing visas to single Christian males.

At one time, the Lebanese population was comprised mainly of Maronite Christians with Muslims and Druze in the minority. When Lebanon gained its independence from France in 1943, the constitution was drafted with this in mind, assigning the presidency post to a Maronite Christian and the prime minister to a Muslim. During the war and with the mass exodus of Christians from the country, the balance shifted in favor of the Muslims, making them

The Burning Cedars

the majority. Christians, however, remained adamant against giving up the presidency and this further ignited the flames of the civil war. For several days, my uncle remained in his room, brooding and miserable. I had no intention of leaving my uncle behind and I told him this, which made him feel a little better about this ordeal. If he was to return to Beirut, I was willing to go back with him although I knew my parents would never allow such an arrangement.
I felt that he cannot he left alone, especially in his condition.

My grandmother had already been living with her sister in South Carolina for some time and knew nothing of what was taking place in Egypt.

Three days went by and my uncle was beginning to gradually accept the fact that he will not be granted a visa. My parents and brother had every intention to go the America and I was to come with them, whether I wanted to or not. Uncle Tony started planning his return to Beirut and with his share of the money from the sale of the building, he wanted to buy a place in a remote part of the country where he could live in relative safety.

For the first time I was to be separated from my uncle. He had always been there for me and now, there was little I could do to be there for him. He felt that we are abandoning him and in a way, he was right, but we had no other options. My parents were doing what was best for us and my uncle just got lost in the shuffle. I wondered with this forced separation if I would ever see my uncle again.

RAMZY BAROODY

The Burning Cedars

CHAPTER FIFTY-FIVE

ARRIVING IN NEW YORK

As it turned out, leaving my uncle behind was not meant to be and the wonderful news came a few days later. My uncle was called into the American embassy for his interview. He came back from the embassy around one pm that day beaming, with a huge happy smile: "I'm coming with you," he screamed after leaping out of the taxi. He flew up the steps and stormed into the apartment jumping up and down screaming over and over again: "I'm coming with you, I'm coming with you."

Not only did my uncle obtain a visa, but one given only to journalists. His was open-ended meaning he can stay in the US for as long as he wishes. The wait for his visa was well worth it, and he was ecstatic. I was so glad to see him happy, I started crying. Not only could I not stand the thought of leaving him behind, I could not imagine living anywhere without him being with me. We packed our belongings so fast that we had to live out of our suitcases for a whole week while my dad was making our travel arrangements. We could not wait to begin our journey and our final week in Egypt just flew by as we planned big and dreamed of a better life. Six months after arriving in Egypt, we were on a plane to New York City. We had an overnight layover at Heathrow airport in England, then on to NY.

My first impression of NY was of uncertainty and bewilderment. A new country, unfamiliar surroundings and too much of everything disoriented all of us.

We stayed at a nice hotel not far from Time Square but we ventured out very infrequently. Our first trip was to the Empire state building, where my uncle wrote his name on the wall of the observation deck, next to thousands of other names written by people from all over the world.

On our way back to the hotel, we stopped at a little souvenir shop and I purchased a small "piggy bank" in the shape of snoopy the dog sleeping on his doghouse. I was unfamiliar with American currency so when it was time to pay, I just handed the lady all the money I had in my pocket and told her to take out what she needed. The store was full of mugs and bumper stickers with the slogan "I ♥ NY." For months I was puzzled by this slogan and wondered what it meant. It wasn't until many months later that I saw an ad on TV with the same slogan along with the song "I love New York" that it dawned on me.

My dad had planned to get into the import/export business and NY was the hub for such an undertaking. We contacted a Lebanese acquaintance that had been living there and asked him to show us the best place where we could live and buy a house. He said Brooklyn had a large Lebanese community and on Sunday, he drove us there to look for houses.

The Burning Cedars

As we drove through the neighborhood, disappointment with the area was evident on all our faces. The Lebanese guy noticed this so he interjected: "It would take you some time to get used to living in this city. Perhaps NY is not the best place for you to settle in right now. It's a big country with lots of options. Take some time and look around before deciding on where you want to live." The narrow streets of Brooklyn were lined on both sides with old row homes, clustered together into one continuous strip of bricks and mortar and with the exception of a few people walking their dogs, the streets seemed desolate in comparison to the hustle and bustle of the Cairo or Beirut streets. A few trees had been planted along the sidewalk, otherwise, the city lacked the greenery and charm we had hoped for. The overcast gray skies, typical of the northeast, magnified the area's lack of appeal and we made our decision to explore other areas more suitable to our needs.

RAMZY BAROODY

The Burning Cedars

CHAPTER FIFTY SIX

ON TO PHILADELPHIA

We stayed in New York for four weeks after which we decided to relocate south to the Philadelphia region. We boarded the Amtrak train and made the two and a half hour trip to 30th Street station in Philadelphia. From there we took a taxi to our hotel, the lovely Benjamin Franklin Hotel in the heart of the city.

It was a cold and overcast day in March of 1979 when we checked into the hotel. The impressive lobby with its large columns wowed everyone and we were anxious to check into our rooms then explore the hotel and the city. Using the tourist city map from the lobby, we walked around for hours visiting the historical sites including the liberty bell, Betsy Ross house, the art museum and Rittenhouse square. Nothing, however, impressed us more than being able to feed the squirrels in the park! The little furry critters came right up to us snatching peanuts out of our hands while we wasted many rolls of film capturing them in action as they frantically borrowed them under leaves or in tree crevasses. Every afternoon my brother and I bought our peanuts from the corner store and headed to the park to feed the squirrels and the pigeons. Early every morning my uncle and I would go downstairs to the restaurant for breakfast. We had a favorite waitress who approached our table with the same inquiry daily: "Sanka? yes? no?." She said this so many times that I started to imitate her endlessly everywhere we went, and my uncle would laugh out loud saying that I sounded just like her.

Although we were enjoying our hotel stay, after one month it was time to find an apartment to settle in. Uncle Eddy (not my real uncle but that's what I called him), a prominent lawyer in the town of Media, a suburb of Philadelphia, who was married to my dad's cousin of the South Carolina Baroody's, volunteered to be our guide.

The first apartment we looked at was in the Society Hill Towers, three upscale high-rise buildings by the Schulkyl River in Philadelphia. The apartment was on the twelfth floor in one of the towers with great panoramic views. It was a sunny yet small place, and for a lot of money so my dad would not go for it.

Uncle Eddy then suggested moving out of the city where apartments are less expensive and the following day he drove us to a delightful town on the outskirts of the city called Drexel Hill. Drexel Brook apartments were charming two-story white buildings scattered among rolling hills on quiet streets with lots of old trees and open spaces. We instantly fell in love with the area and within one week, we moved into a second floor two bedroom, one bath, walk-up apartment. My uncle rented an adjacent place of a similar configuration and prepared for my grandmother to come up from South Carolina and live with him.

The Burning Cedars

We wasted no time in settling down and enjoying our new life in this quiet and peaceful neighborhood. My bedroom window overlooked some large acorn trees populated by a family of adorable black squirrels. They used to come right up to the window and snatch food out of my hand, and then run back to a branch where they frantically chewed on it with such energy and speed. The way squirrels eat is so comical to me, as if someone was winding them up from behind then letting them go crazy.

At the end of our street was the Drexel Brooke club. For a modest fee you can purchase a seasonal membership, which entitled you to use the restaurant and the large pool in the back. My brother and I took full advantage of our memberships and during the hot and humid summer months went swimming every afternoon along with hundreds of other families who resided nearby.

RAMZY BAROODY

1979 - At a park in downtown Philadelphia.

I enjoyed feeding the pigeons and the squirrels in the afternoon while my parents searched for an apartment.

The Burning Cedars

CHAPTER FIFTY-SEVEN

THE FLOOD

One Monday afternoon in the summer of 1979, my uncle came over to our house fuming with anger, cursing the day he came to America. He said he was shaving and left the water running in the bathroom. The sink overflowed and flooded the downstairs apartment. Mrs. Zigmond, the downstairs tenant became furious, screaming and yelling at my uncle and grandmother.

We walked back to my uncle's apartment to investigate and saw Mrs. Zigmond hauling most of her belongings, including furniture and clothing out onto the front lawn. She was claiming that everything was ruined by the "flood." The apartment manager was called and after inspecting both apartments, decided that my uncle and grandmother should be moved to another apartment while the management company assesses and repairs the water damage.

A few days later, my uncle received a certified letter in the mail. As he read it, his face turned pure white and began to shake with anger: "That bitch is suing us for damages," he said, "She's actually suing us for ruining her crappy furniture and her clothes."

My uncle was fit to be tied and began cursing Mrs. Zigmond and the day he came to this country. He grabbed the letter

The Burning Cedars

and ran to show my dad, who then called Uncle Eddy who in turn told them to bring the letter to his law office right away. Uncle Eddy assured them that he will take care of everything and they have nothing to worry about, which pleased my uncle.

Several weeks went by and no one heard anything about the lawsuit, so we called uncle Eddy: "I took care of her," he told us, "I sent her a stern letter and spoke to her over the phone. She is dropping her lawsuit."

We were all greatly relieved by the news and tried to put this incident behind us. All except my uncle who was deeply hurt and disappointed by what he had to go through. He was never able to let go of this incident and for many months to follow, he mentioned Mrs. Zigmond and the lawsuit incessantly to anyone willing to listen.

He was also unhappy with his new surroundings and could not acclimate himself to the "American way of life." He found their actions, culture, associations with one another, way of speaking and expressing themselves unfamiliar and awkward and he began to regret moving to America and yearned to go back home to Lebanon.

RAMZY BAROODY

The Burning Cedars

CHAPTER FIFTY-EIGHT

THE PET ADOPTION CENTER

At fifteen, the transition to a new country with a diverse society was easier for me to adjust to than for my uncle and parents. I was able to gradually acclimate myself to my new surroundings and with the exception of a pronounced accent and Middle Eastern looks, I embraced and celebrated my new way of life and tried to blend in as much as possible.

Watching all the dog walkers on my street, I decided that my first course of action to "blend in" was to get a dog. I have always been a cat lover but it seemed like owning a dog was the thing to do in America. After all, dogs are great companions and I valued their loyalty, good nature and the sense of security they provided.

"I want a dog," I told my uncle

"You don't know anything about taking care of dogs my love," he replied. "You need to walk them, bathe them, take them to a vet if they get sick. Dogs are high maintenance. Are you willing to take on such a responsibility?"

"I am bored with nothing to do all day and a dog will keep me company," I replied. He then assured me that the next day we will go and *look* at some dogs.

Upon hearing the news, my mom did not waste any time voicing her objections to owning "a filthy disgusting beast running around the house," and made it clear that she will not clean up after it. "We're just going to look," I replied.

The next day, aunt Elizabeth, my grandmother's American cousin who was a dog lover and owner herself, picked us up in her station wagon and drove us to the local animal shelter, the Media SPCA.

On our way out of the house, my mom intercepted us with a stern reminder: "Remember, you're just going to look!""Yes yes we remember," I answered, then I repeated everything she told us the previous day, word for word, "You don't want those filthy disgusting beasts in the house and you will not clean up after them."

The town of Media's SPCA is situated on a hill overlooking a pet cemetery. We got out of the car and I took a stroll through the cemetery to read what pet owners had inscribed on the tombstones of their dead pets: "In loving memory" read one inscription, and "Fluffy I love you as much as I love my children," and "Max we'll never forget you - RIP."

My personal favorite was "You are in heaven now - we will see you soon." That was quite odd and disturbing, I told my uncle as I walked back.

Aunt Elizabeth had some errands to take care of so she dropped us off at the SPCA and left.

The Burning Cedars

We walked through the adoption area where dozens of cats and dogs sadly waited for their would-be new owners to rescue them. The caretaker brought some of the animals out of their cages to play with us and I adored a beautiful Alaskan Husky with blue eyes, who jumped up and down, wagging his blue tail furiously at the chance of being adopted. "He's way too big for you," my uncle commented, and so we continued our walk. Next they brought out an adorable, one year-old dog of a mixed breed of Golden Retriever. I instantly fell in love with this one and decided that this is the dog I wanted. "Your mother will be furious if we brought a dog back," my uncle reminded me.

"But I want this dog, please.." I begged. Within the hour, they were prepping my dog for adoption and after his flee dip, we walked out the proud owners of a beautiful, and extremely hyper Golden Retriever mix. There was only one problem now-we had no way to get home.

RAMZY BAROODY

The Burning Cedars

CHAPTER FIFTY-NINE

THE LONG WALK HOME

Lebanon is a small country and people got around on foot as much as possible. Unfamiliar with the vastness of the States and underestimating the distances between towns and cities, we unwisely determined that we could walk home from the adoption center.

Route One, a major six-lane highway connects Media to Drexel Brooke, a distance of about eight miles. With the dog in tow, my uncle and I jumped over the metal highway barricade and began our walk. Cars dashed by at top speed as we were being pummeled by dirt and dust and breathing in toxic fumes. In the far distant loomed an overpass and we were confident that this was the Drexel Brooke exit. Another hour's walk and we reached the overpass which was the Springfield exit. Sproul Road/route 320 led to Springfield Mall, and we were still over four miles away from home. "What shall we do now," I asked my uncle who was equally lost, confused and frustrated. "Let's hitchhike," he answered. So there we were, a man, a kid and a dog hitchhiking on the side of the road. Hundreds of cars drove past and none stopped to help us. After a while, with every car that drove past, my uncle would turn around and give them the finger. To keep me occupied, my uncle invented what he called the "hitchhikers' finger": "look," he said laughing nervously "After each car that goes by, I will slowly turn around while switching fingers from my thumb to my middle finger."

His little game wore thin very rapidly and with no foreseeable resolution to our predicament, we had to find a way to get back home, and fast.

Throughout all this, my poor frightened, exhausted and dehydrated dog sat calmly by my side, most likely thinking to himself "What did I get myself into?. Of all the people in this town, these two idiots had to adopt me! I was better off at the shelter."

When the hitchhiking method failed, we had but one option remaining: find a bus to take us home. We were unfamiliar with designated bus stops and their routes so the next bus we spotted, we frantically waved our arms in the air to get the driver's attention. He must have recognized the look of despair and lack of common sense so he stopped.

We desperately pleaded with the driver to take us to Drexel brook, which fortunately was on his designated route, but there was a problem. He was not allowed to have dogs on the bus other than the ones used by visually impaired people. After begging and pleading with him for over ten minutes, to the angry stares of his passengers, he finally acquiesced.

On our way home, we knew that we had a bigger problem waiting for us once we got there. "Your mother is going to hit the roof when she sees what we have brought with us," my uncle reminded me.

The Burning Cedars

CHAPTER SIXTY

WELCOMING THE DOG HOME

We finally arrived at home, exhausted, frustrated and covered in dirt and road grime. I asked my uncle to walk in first and with a big smile on his face, to announce that we have a surprise for everyone. My thinking was that this would prepare my parents for what I was about to spring on them. At least, that was what I hoped for, but in reality I knew they were going to hit the roof, especially when they specifically told me not to get a dog.

I stood at the bottom of the stairs as my nervous uncle made the announcement. There was dead silence in the room and I'm thinking this is not a good sign. As I started to slowly walk up the stairs, my dog slipped away from me and bolted into the room, tail furiously wagging, he climbed on top of everyone in uncontrollable excitement. My uncle and I both froze in place, speechless and fearful for our lives.

Then the most unexpected and wonderful thing happened. I looked around the room and everyone was beaming, purely delighted with this hairy beast mauling and nibbling at them. My mom was the first to break the uncomfortable silence: "He's adorable," she said with

The Burning Cedars

a big smile on her face. Then she proceeded to inquire as to how we managed to get him home, where we got him from and so on, so I told her the whole story of our hitchhiking adventure and having to walk on the highway for miles, but she heard none of it, occupied with the dog as he continued his joyful spasms, jumping up and down and forcing himself on top of everyone. After he was finished with his "welcome home" tantrum, my dog decided that my mothers' lap was to be his sleeping quarters and there's where he rested, with his head on her thigh and those adorable puppy eyes.

As with most dogs, being excited or engaging in physical activity causes them to emit a slight "doggy odor", which my mom quickly picked up on.

"We have to bathe him," she insisted. "Put him in the bathtub and I will be in to help you in a minute." Once I had him securely in the tub, my mom walked in with a bottle of Tide Laundry detergent-Lavender and Linen scented. "You hold him while I scrub him," she said, "Tide will clean him up nicely."

I didn't know much about raising dogs but I knew that you couldn't wash an animal in Tide. "You can't use that on him," I objected, "It'll kill him."

"Oh he'll be fine," my mother declared, "I wash everything in Tide."

"Did you ever bathe us in Tide when we were kids?" I asked her. "No" she answered unconvincingly, "But I used to wipe you down with rubbing alcohol after giving you a bath!"

"Don't use Tide on the dog and don't rub him down with alcohol either" I said, "we have to get him dog shampoo."

During the time my mom and I were having this conversation, the dog was getting very restless in the bathtub, probably again thinking "what did I get myself into with this crazy family?"

I told my mom to take him out of the tub while I went to the store with my uncle to buy dog shampoo. On our way there, we were both having second thoughts as to my mom's sincerity in not bathing the dog with Tide. Half way to the store, we both looked at each other and without saying another word, ran back home to check on the dog.

Luckily my mom was busy mopping the floor with the Tide she had intended for the dog, so we grabbed him and ran to the store for his shampoo.

The Burning Cedars

CHAPTER SIXTY-ONE

TRIALS AND TRIBULATIONS OF DOG OWNERSHIP

*N*ow that I have a dog, it was time to name him. I went through several choices before deciding on a name that best fits his tempestuous personality "Ruff Ruff."

I took Ruff Ruff everywhere I went while disregarding his untrained behavior and disobedient disposition. He chased other dogs, jumped on people in the street, did his business anywhere he felt like it, and on several occasions, wiggled his way out of his collar and took off running down the street into traffic and other peoples' yards.

His ultimate act of disobedience was fully played out at the local supermarket. My uncle and I took him with us food shopping at the local *Shop n' Bag* supermarket. Ruff Ruff and I waited outside while my uncle went in to buy some groceries. Within ten minutes, Ruff Ruff managed to squirm out of his leash and took off into the store, running up and down the isles, molesting everyone in his path.

Within a few seconds, he managed to disappear with nowhere in sight as I ran up and down every isle trying to locate him. Along the way, I ran into my uncle and told him what had happened, who in turn dropped his groceries and took off running throughout the

The Burning Cedars

supermarket screaming at the op of his lungs "Ruff Ruff come back!" to the stares and snickers of the other shoppers. Fifteen minutes passed and Ruff Ruff was nowhere to be found. Patrons of the store were telling us they had seen him running around from one isle to the next, but after and exhaustive search, we could not locate him anywhere.

It then occurred to me that he might have managed to leave the store so I ran outside in a panic hoping he did not run into traffic on the main road. Meanwhile, my uncle continued to search for him inside, yelling "Ruff Ruff come back" as people stared and shook their heads in disbelief.

Finally after several minutes of this fiasco, we saw Ruff Ruff in the arms of the store butcher as they were heading our way: "I assume this is what you're looking for," the butcher said. Ruff Ruff had made his way all the way to the back of the store, through the meat department and into the back room where they trim and package the meats. Luckily, the butcher was a kind old man who loved dogs and was pleasantly surprised by my dog's uninvited visit and self-administered tour of the store. "He's a cute dog," the butcher added, "but you have to tighten his collar so that he can't wiggle his way out of it next time."

Embarrassed by his unruly behavior, I grabbed my euphorically energized dog with tail wagging at an uncontrollable speed, and ran out of the store with my uncle. It was shortly after this incident, and hearing my uncle's calls of "Ruff Ruff come back" when I decided to rename my dog. Nothing was more embarrassing than to hear a grown man calling his dog "Ruff Ruff!"

I renamed my dog "Whiskey" mostly because of the resemblance in color to the intoxicating drink and also because my dog Whiskey sometimes acted as if he has had one-too-many drinks. All this excitement caused Whiskey to have a bad case of diarrhea the day after. What was worse, he had a few accidents inside the apartment, sending my mother into a hysterical cleaning frenzy, but this was not the worst of it. It was when I came home that day and found my mother with surgical gloves on her hands chasing whiskey around the house with paper towels.

"What is going on?" I asked.

"Your dog is shitting all over himself then sitting on the carpet, so I've been wiping his ass with soap and water," she answered nonchalantly.

"Have you been wiping his ass with Tide?" I asked.

Again, she answered unconvincingly, "NO, just soap and water on a paper towel," as if wiping the dog's ass with plain soap rather than Tide is any less disturbing.

This charade went on for three days with my mom chasing after Whiskey with the paper towels every time he did his business. Finally, Whiskey recovered physically from his diarrhea yet I am certain my mother had scarred him mentally for a long time!

The Burning Cedars

CHAPTER SIXTY-TWO

A SAD GOODBYE

By June of 1979, my brother and I were getting bored and restless of sitting around with nothing to do. My dad suggested that we should enroll in some classes which will occupy our time and prepare us for the upcoming fall school year. I enrolled in the "English as a second language" summer course offered at the Lansdown Avenue high school. I took the local trolley to the Lansdown avenue stop then walked to school. Shucry enrolled in a business course at Widener, a private university in Chester, PA, a half hour bus ride from our house.

Although my class was designed for students with little to no prior education in the English language, I enjoyed getting out of the house and meeting other foreign students from around the world. My uncle walked me to the trolley stop daily and was waiting for me when I got home in the afternoon.

Throughout my earlier education in Lebanon, I have received a solid foundation in the English language and learned little from this summer class, yet I did pick up on the American slang and the different ways of pronouncing and forming sentences. My first day of class, I was asked to spell my name, and I replied " R, A, M, Zed, Y."

The Burning Cedars

Everyone looked at me in bewilderment and the teacher corrected me saying: "In this country we say Z not Zed. That's the British way of pronouncing things."

Other than managing to export a few clothing containers back to Beirut, my dad was beginning to get restless and bored as well. He needed a full-time job to occupy his time and that offer came in September of 1979.

My dad's business partner called him from Beirut asking him to come back. He said the war was under control and things are improving. Life was returning to normal, shops are opening back up and they are busier than ever distributing goods to stores and warehouses. My dad jumped at the opportunity and began arranging his return as quickly as possible. The plan was for him to go back and work in Beirut while we stayed behind in America. He will send us money regularly to cover all expenses and in a year or so, if all goes well, we will join him there.

My dad had been in Beirut for exactly one month when he started calling daily insisting that we return. He said the war had ended and he plans on staying there permanently. A few days went by and my dad began to sense our hesitation in returning to Lebanon so quickly. He then decided to threaten cutting off all money transfers unless we return immediately.

Initially, my mom and I were resistant to going back, skeptical of the so-called cease-fire and remembering all the broken ones from years past.

My uncle was homesick and wanted to go back so he and my grandmother were proceeding with the preparation to return.

My grandmother did not care one way or another, perhaps because she knew that at the first sign of hostilities, she would be on a plane to her sister in South Carolina.

My brother was apprehensive yet amenable. Although skeptical of the cease-fire, he was also homesick and eager to return. At the end, we had no choice but to agree to go back.

The most difficult part of having to return was leaving my beloved dog, Whiskey, behind. We have all grown very attached to this little hell raiser and the thought of never seeing him again deeply saddened me.

Aunt Elizabeth again drove us to the Media SPCA where we had adopted Whiskey six months earlier so that we can take care of the somber and unpleasant task of returning him.

Whiskey did not know what was planned for him and happily wagged his tail, content to be in the car with the rest of us.

My mom and I were crying hysterically and when we arrived, we stood in the parking lot for our final goodbye and took a farewell Polaroid picture of Whiskey by the front entrance of the SPCA, the only picture I had of my beloved dog before having to give him up. I never saw him again after that day.

The Burning Cedars

CHAPTER SIXTY-THREE

BACK WHERE WE STARTED FROM-ALMOST

*W*e returned to Lebanon in late October, 1979. My dad was waiting for us at the airport and said he had a surprise for us. We got into the taxi and began our ascend up into the hills surrounding Beirut. Fifteen minutes later, the taxi veered left off the Beirut-Damascus highway into *Louaizeh,* a quaint little town on a hill overlooking Beirut and the Mediterranean.

The location of this town was ideal for several reasons. It was nestled in an alcove bordered by hills on the north and south sides and rolling ravines to the west stretching down to Beirut. The fresh crisp Mediterranean Sea air channeled swiftly through the hills and over our town made for brisk and balmy summers and tepid and snow-free winters. Also, in this town is where my Aunt Mona, my mothers' youngest sister, lived with her family. Her house was on a cliff overlooking our apartment only a few yards away, close enough for me to be able to carry a conversation from my bedroom balcony with my aunt or her son, Daniel; that is if you didn't mind letting all the neighbors in on your personal business!

The Burning Cedars

The taxi pulled up in front of a newly constructed building at the edge of town where my dad had rented an apartment. It was a beautiful and picturesque western-facing two bedroom apartment on the second floor.

From our balconies, we enjoyed uninterrupted views of Beirut, the sea and surrounding villages with their redbrick roof houses scattered among the pine and olive trees. I shared a bedroom with my brother while my mom and dad slept in the master.

My uncle and grandmother stayed with us for a very short time until they bought their own apartment in the town of *Hazmieh*, a suburb of Beirut about two miles west of Louaizeh. Their apartment was within walking distance of *Dar-Assayad*, the newspaper and magazine publishers where my uncle worked.

With my dad and uncle back at work, it was time for my brother and me to continue our education.

My brother enrolled in the B.U.C. (Beirut University College) majoring in Business and Accounting. To get back and forth to college, my dad bought him a *Renault*, which he drove around town proudly as it was his first car.

I needed two more years of high school to graduate, and one Monday morning in early November, my dad and I drove to a private British high school south of Beirut by the name *Eastwood College*.

The Lebanese system of education is modeled after the French system where a student completes his Freshman and Sophomore classes in high school rather than college as is the case in the US, prior to moving on to University. Furthermore, the school year in Lebanon runs from November till June and I was able to enroll at Eastwood just in time for the start of the school year. I lived outside the school bus zone so they arranged for a special driver to pick me up every morning from my house.

On the first day of school, a yellow station wagon pulled up outside the house and I said my goodbyes to my parents and walked out. As I approached the car I realized it was full of children. The only vacant seat was in the front next to the driver, so I opened the door and jumped in. I was immediately taken back by what I saw. The car was filthy with food crumbs and stains all over the seats and carpet and the source of this filth was sitting next to me.

The Burning Cedars

1980 - On the balcony of our apartment in Louaizeh.
*Enjoying the sun, the view and being back in Lebanon.
(from left) My brother, me, cousin Daniel.*

*The view from my bedroom balcony looking north.
Snow-capped Mount Sannin can be seen in the far distant.*

RAMZY BAROODY

*Our apartment afforded breathtaking panoramic views
of the Mediterranean sea, Beirut and surrounding hills and mountains.*

The Burning Cedars

CHAPTER SIXTY-FOUR

EASTWOOD COLLEGE

The school cab driver's son, a mentally retarded ten-year-old boy sat in the center front seat wedged between his father and me. He suffered from Mongolism, which today is referred to as Down syndrome. The kid's name was John and he was unable to speak, only grunts and mumbles, had no teeth so when he ate most of the food ended up on the floor or me. Had very poor hygiene and when he had to go to the bathroom, he did not hesitate to do so in the car.

He also suffered from behavioral and anger issues, frequently throwing tantrums or thrashing about in his seat. John also suffered from difficulty in breathing and had flu-like symptoms constantly. When he sneezed or coughed (which he did often), phlegm and spit flew out of his nose and mouth bathing everyone nearby.

John's special needs school was on our way to Eastwood, so his father saw fit that he should bring him along with the rest of the Eastwood students, drop him off in the morning at his school then pick him up at the end of the day. What's more, I was the last student on this route to be picked up in the morning and given that none of the other kids wanted to sit upfront, they all piled up almost on top of each other in the back leaving the only available seat right beside John.

The Burning Cedars

I have always thought that an ignorant person is one who lacks the proper knowledge, understanding or education of a particular situation or issue. Coupled with naivety and unfamiliarity with a certain ailment or disability, I faced the daily agonizing and challenging dilemma of dealing with a child whose disability frightened and appalled me. Through no fault of his own and because of my own shortcomings and preconceptions about Down syndrome, I, along with the other kids in that car, managed to shun and rebuke this kid, isolating and condemning him based on our own fears and misunderstandings.

While John's behavior and actions were abnormal, I managed to exasperate the situation to the point of refusing to go to school or ride in the same car with this kid anymore. I complained constantly until my uncle finally agreed to take me to school and pick me up daily, and that's what we did.

Similar to Beirut Evangelical, Eastwood College was founded and run by British Evangelical missionaries. It was located in a converted six story residential building in the southern suburb of Beirut. Next to the building was an outdoor swimming pool which was opened once the weather got warmer and during our designated Friday afternoon Physical Education classes, we would put on our swimming trunks and jump into the still icy-cold water while trying to avoid the flying divers as they bounced off the diving board, half the time landing on top of their classmates in the pool.

Apart from the rigorous academic program and the strict British teachers, I enjoyed my new school and did very well academically. English and Science were my favorite subjects while Arabic was my least favorite. Other subjects we studied included Math, History, Geography, Religion and Physical Education. I obtained mostly A's and B's for the 1979-1980 academic year and was advanced to the next grade for the 1980-1981 year. Most surprisingly, however, was my uncharacteristic accomplishment of befriending everyone in my class. I had always been the well liked yet shy kid in the school, but at Eastwood, I became the popular, funny and outspoken student I had always yearned to become. Somehow I managed to instill my sense of humor and easy-going nature into my association with others and this worked out flawlessly. I finally achieved what I had struggled with accomplishing my entire life and I liked it. My classmates refused to go on class trips unless I came along and in those days before emails and cell phones, friends dropped by my house constantly to check up on me and some even wrote me letters when I missed classes because of an illness. The school year went by quickly and joyously and I looked forward to the following year, not anticipating a sudden illness, which will send me to the hospital and keep me away from my friends and school for several months to come.

The Burning Cedars

CHAPTER SIXTY FIVE

HEPATITIS

*O*ne late afternoon in October, 1980, I was in the bathroom at home when I felt extremely weak and lightheaded. Next thing I remember, I was on the bathroom floor with my mom and aunt Mona in a panic trying to revive me. I managed to get back on my feet but felt very faint and incoherent. My mom helped me to my bed and there I stayed until my dad came home that night and noticed that my eyes and skin had a yellow tint to them.

Early the following morning, I was driven to our family doctor in Beirut who diagnosed me as having Jaundice as a result of Hepatitis and an inflamed liver. He said the most probable cause was drinking contaminated water. In Lebanon homes are supplied with two sources of water - drinking water that is (allegedly) filtered and treated and non-drinking water used for bathing, laundry and other non-consumable tasks. The doctor said that drinking water is at times polluted with pathogens and that was likely the source of my illness.

I was confined to bed for over one month and although I was in no physical pain, the yellowing of my skin and eyes lingered for weeks then gradually began to dissipate.

The Burning Cedars

Throughout this time, I missed the first few weeks of the new school year and no one bothered to inform the school administration of my illness. Meanwhile, letters and phone calls from my classmates flooded the house. Some questioned my whereabouts while others who knew of my illness wished me a speedy recovery. Others updated me on what I have been missing at school, passing along all the gossip about the students and teachers. One day there was a knock at the door and when I answered, the schools' principle, Ms. Singin Smyth along with one of the teachers were standing in the doorway. They have made the trip to check in on me and see how I was doing. I was taken back by their act of kindness and well wishing and told them I will return as soon as the doctor allows me to do so.

It was another three weeks before I was allowed to return to school. I walked in Monday morning during our Arabic lesson and the entire class stood up and cheered.
My face turned as red as a ripe tomato and I was speechless. I never expected this kind of a reception and was truly touched and grateful for my classmates' compassion and support. Having missed so many school days, I initially struggled to catch up with my studies. My teachers and classmates were understanding and supportive, helping me in every way they could.

My brother was also doing well at University and was a few courses away from obtaining his Baccalaureate degree. My uncle and grandmother were busy furnishing their new apartment and my grandmother bought a new organ which she played almost daily but particularly on Sunday playing her favorite church songs. Things were going well for everyone and as the political situation remained calm, we gradually settled in and began rebuilding our lives slowly yet surely.

The Burning Cedars

CHAPTER SIXTY-SIX

A SUDDEN AND VIOLENT ASSAULT

By January, 1981, the second installment of my school tuition was due. My dad and I drove down and met with one of the school counselors who gave me a list of the required books I needed to buy for the new semester, my class schedule and other school supplies needed.

My dad then reached into his pocket and pulled out One Thousand Lebanese Liras in cash and handed them over to the counselor as payment for the school year. At that moment, we heard a loud explosion which shook the building followed by a constant barrage of gunfire. Shortly after, more explosions and gunfire and we hurried down to the basement. We had no clue as to what was going on (yet feared the worst) and after half an hour, the gunfire tapered off and we rushed into my dad's car and drove home at top speed. Other than military vehicles patrolling the neighborhoods, the streets were empty of cars and we arrived at home that afternoon to discover that my mom and brother were nowhere to be found. We could hear gunfire and explosions from Beirut and my dad and I stood outside waiting and worrying about my mom and brother.

The Burning Cedars

Several hours went by and it was getting dark yet no one has seen or heard from either my brother or mother. Suddenly it occurred to me that it was Tuesday, the day when Jehovah's Witnesses have their meetings and that is most likely where they had been. What is worse is that the meetings were conducted in Aley, our old hometown that is now predominantly Druze. Aley was a half hour drive up the mountain from our home off the Beirut-Damascus highway which, according to the news, has been shut down due to the ensuing fighting.

Seven pm and still no sight of my mom or brother and by now my dad and I were hysterical with worry. I told my dad perhaps they had gone to my aunt Violet's house, which was in the neighboring village to stay with her until the roads re-open. From our apartment we could see the Beirut-Damascus highway in the distant and I stood on the balcony looking out for any cars that resemble my brothers'.
My dad continued to walk in and out of the apartment, standing in the middle of the street praying they come home safely. Shortly afterwards I joined him outside and as we stood there, a barrage of rockets fired from the vicinity of Aley flew directly over our heads on their way to East Beirut.

The Syrian army had resumed their assault on the Christian neighborhoods and we were caught in the middle, again. There was a Syrian army outpost not a mile from our house and they were hastily preparing to join in the fighting. I watched them as they removed the camouflage covers off their tanks and prepared them for firing. Army men frantically ran in and out of their barricades carrying guns and rocket propellers and taking their positions on the surrounding hills. They seemed to be as un-prepared and startled by the sudden outbreak of fighting as we were.

As we stood outside waiting, we could hear new and more powerful sounds and explosions like we've never heard before. The Syrian army was using larger and more powerful guns and multi-rocket propellers in shelling East Beirut. Multiple rockets streaked the sky overhead on their way to Beirut, and one barrage flew by so low that we were almost knocked to the ground by the powerful current they generated.

My dad and I ran inside but felt just as exposed and vulnerable as we did outside. Our apartment directly overlooked East Beirut and any misguided retaliation placed us directly in the crossfire.

It was now nine o'clock and I continued to periodically peek out our kitchen balcony looking for my brothers' car as the rockets continued to fly overhead. My dad and I huddled in the kitchen, which was in the back of the house facing east, away from Beirut. Suddenly I heard the roaring of a car engine and saw two dim deadlights coming up the street-It was them. As my brother approached the house, he turned off his car headlights so that he cannot be seen from Beirut and mistaken for a Syrian target.

They pulled up and rushed into the house looking stressed and scared. As I suspected, they had been at the Jehovah's Witnesses meeting in Aley when the fighting started. They ended the meeting early due to the sudden outbreak in the fighting but were unable to leave the hall for several hours.

The Burning Cedars

When the fighting subsided, they were told the highway had been shut down. They had to wind their way home down the mountainside on traitorous back roads through Druze and Muslim villages until finally, over three hours later, they made it home. My mom was hysterical and my brother hardly said a word. He just looked around glassy eyed and panic stricken. We told them that missiles had been flying directly overhead and it would be unsafe and unwise to stay in the house.

Up till then, the shelling had been one sided with no retaliation from the Christian militias. Most likely they were caught off guard by this swift and violent onslaught and as shocked as the rest of us. As far as anyone knew, there had been no signs or basis for this offensive yet none of us knew what was taking place behind the scenes, and whatever that was, it could not have ended amicably between the fighting factions.

That night we stayed in our house as the rockets continued to fly overhead and early the next morning, we decided to go to my mom's sister, aunt Violet's place in a secluded and relatively safe village in the mountains. My uncle and grandmother stayed behind in their apartment in Beirut.

Aunt Violet was a kind and easy going woman who married a strange and eccentric man and they lived with his mother in a large house in a village not too far from Aley. Her husband was the type of person who no matter what topic of conversation you discussed with him, he took the opposite view and argued with you for hours trying to convince you that he was right. His mother was as strange as he was, yet they both had one redeeming value-they both loved my aunt and treated her with the respect and appreciation she deserved.

We arrived at Aunt Violet's house late that afternoon bringing with us a gallon of olive oil as a token of our appreciation for letting us stay with them. They welcomed us with open arms, particularly the mother-in-law, who told us to consider their house ours and to stay as long as we liked.

But later that night, my mom discovered that the old lady had a dark and sinister side which she had kept well hidden from everyone until the sun went down.

The Burning Cedars

CHAPTER SIXTY-SEVEN

THE NIGHTLY VISITOR

Our first night at Aunt Violet we went to bed around midnight. Shortly after, my mom was awakened by voices of two people in the next room carrying on a loud and heated conversation. My mom got out of bed and tip toed towards the mother-in-law's room where the voices were coming from. All the lights in the room were turned off yet she was clearly having an argument with someone inside. My mom stood at the door and listened in: "These people came to our house uninvited, they forced themselves on us and now we're stuck with them" the mother-in-law said.

"When do you think they're leaving?" asked the other person.

"I have no idea," answered the mother-in-law, "All they brought with them is a gallon of olive oil and now we're stuck with them for God-knows how long. What's more, the Syrian army will now come to the house and take us all away."

This back-and-forth dialogue continued for over an hour and although some of it was incomprehensible, the topic of conversation was unmistakable: our presence was unwelcome.

My mom was very upset by what she heard and curious to find out who the other person in the room was, so she cracked the door

The Burning Cedars

open slowly and carefully and peeked in but was unable to see anything. So she decided to go out onto the balcony and peek in through the open bedroom window but again was unable to see anything. So she went back into the house and stood at the bedroom door. The room was dark except for a small nightlight in the corner and the mother-in-law was sitting up in bed facing a chair. The heated conversation continued as they both expressed their dissatisfaction with the situation and clearly resented our presence.

My mom quietly and carefully nudged the door slightly open a little more and stuck her head into the room to witness the shock of her life.

The mother-in-law was sitting in bed having a conversation with herself in two distinctly different tones of voices. She would ask a question in one tone then answer herself in another, and this continued non-stop for hours.

My mom was beside herself and ran back to our room waking all of us up. Her face was white as a sheet and she was shaking all over, barely able to speak: "We uh have to..we're leaving..rright now..we're leaving" she kept saying over and over again.

"What's wrong? what's the matter with you?" my dad asked.

"This woman in possessed and she's having a conversation with herself as two people," my mom said, "we're leaving right now."

My mom then proceeded to tell us what she had seen and heard and that she refuses to stay in the same house with this evil woman.

It was now almost two am and there was no way for us to go anywhere at this hour, so my dad assured my mom that everything will be ok and to go to sleep, as he rolled over and started snoring. That night, my mom got no sleep at all, even after the "conversation" in the next room finally ended and hour later.

When morning came and my aunt got up to make us coffee, my mom confronted her in the kitchen with what she had heard and seen the previous night. Rather than showing concern or alarm, my aunt broke out in a long laughter. "She does this every night," my aunt answered casually, "we're used to it."
"How can you get used to this," my mom answered, "this woman is possessed." Again my aunt laughed, "She's not possessed, just deaf. She has no idea that she's talking out loud and she carries conversations with herself every night."

My mom then told my aunt that her mother-in-law was complaining about us being there and wanted us out. "She didn't mean it," my sweet and kind aunt answered, "besides, this is as much my house as it is hers and I want you here regardless."

This calmed down my mother slightly yet she remained on edge in the mother-in-law's company, especially for all the bad things she had said about us staying there. During the day, the mother in law was as kind and sweet as can be and insisted that we stay with them for as long as we like and this is as much our home as it is theirs. Yet at night, her other, perhaps "real" personality was revealed and she wanted us out of the house at any cost.

So we stayed for several more weeks, not that we had much of a choice.

The Burning Cedars

The fighting continued and intensified, the roads were closed and to attempt to go back was impossible. The mother-in-law repeated her rants and raves nightly. The topics of her "conversations" changed daily, from "The Syrian army is coming to kill us," to "when I visited Russia a few years ago I saw all the castles with walls decorated in gold and precious jewels." After a while, we managed to sleep through the night, ignoring the "trip around the world" tour emanating from her room.

Aunt Violet (left) with her mother-in-law who carried out long and heated debates with herself all night long.

The Burning Cedars

CHAPTER SIXTY EIGHT

THE BALANCE OF POWER IS SHIFTED

Over three weeks went by when the fighting subsided enough for us to return home. The town of Louaizeh was almost completely deserted with the exception of my aunt Mona and several neighbors in our building. Luckily, our home did not sustain any direct hits, only several shrapnel and bullet holes in my bedroom wall that did not penetrate all the way through.

The war however, did not come to a complete stop and from our balcony we could see the gunfire streaking in the sky like red lightning bolts back and forth between East and West Beirut nightly.

For over six years now, the war had lingered in one form or another. Most Lebanese had gotten so used to this kind of living that sporadic gunfire and shelling had less of an impact on our daily lives. At daybreak when the fighting subsided, shops and businesses opened and the roads were jammed with cars as people went to work.

Movie theaters re-opened and my brother and I, along with one of my brother's friends went to the movies in Beirut one Sunday to see "The Shining." It was very uncharacteristic of my brother to invite me to go anywhere with him, yet on that day, he did, and I went.

The Burning Cedars

After the movie and as darkness fell, we hurried back home in anticipation of the resumption in fighting.

It was an odd and unreal way of living that at anytime, you could be killed, and yet you lived in the moment, trying to have a normal life as much as possible in the middle of total chaos and destruction. It was like clockwork that every night at sundown, the fighting would resume ending pre-dawn.

My brother was able to continue his education at the University while my school remained closed since it was located in a volatile area dividing the Christian east Beirut from the Muslim west.

Unfortunately, before too long, the fighting intensified again into a twenty-four-hour event and the daytime lull was no more. By then, my brother had finished all his courses and was to receive his BS diploma but was unable to safely get to the University to pick it up.

One day, the fighting had suddenly and mysteriously stopped and my brother was determined to pick up his diploma. He got into his car and made the trip to Beirut. Shortly after leaving, the shelling abruptly resumed, getting wildly intense and violent in a very short period of time. We were all terrified and extremely concerned for my brother, and with no means of knowing his whereabouts, we paced up and down the corridor, praying for his safe return.

Soon after, my brother returned with the diploma in hand yet somehow, it meant little to anyone at this stage. The next morning after spending another sleepless night listening to the sounds of gunfire, the rumble of passing tanks and the roars of explosions, my dad had had enough. Red-eyed, droopy cheeked and with heavy black circles under his eyes from the lack of sleep and frayed nerves, he expressed his total disgust and loss of patience with the situation and this country. He realized that our decision to return to Lebanon so hastily was in error and it was obvious that the war has not, and will not, end anytime soon.

Multiple cease-fires had been implemented then broken while the fundamental cause of this war has not been resolved. It was clear that each faction wanted to dominate the other while the country remained deeply divided along religions affiliations.

Lebanon's population at that time was close to two million and with over twenty distinct and heavily armed militias roaming the streets, each with its own political, religious and ethnic agenda and foreign support, the fractures in our society were deep and wide arriving to a hopeless cause and past the point of reconciliation.

The Muslims, Druze and Palestinians were aligned on one side backed mainly by Syria who supplied them with money, ammunition and its military presence. The Christians were backed by the US and to a lesser extent, Israel. The Christians were outgunned, under funded and less than fully supported by their so-called allies in sharp contrast to the Muslim militias, who had the full dedication and support of their fundamental allies. It was truly a remarkable accomplishment the way the Christians were able to hold their ground and prevent their total demise on the hands of all those who promised to "throw them into the sea in six days."

The Burning Cedars

The Lebanese war managed to destroy most of the country, kill an estimated 200,000 men, women and children and force millions to seek refuge in any country that will accept them. The war did manage to produce one very important outcome - It reversed the balance of power, taking it away from the Christian majority and shifting it to the new majority, the Muslims.

Today Lebanon is nearly 60% Muslim and 40% Christian and the numbers continue to fluctuate yet steadily shifting in favor of the Muslims. The president, although stripped of the greater part of his executive powers, remains a Maronite Christian for the time being.

RAMZY BAROODY

The Burning Cedars

CHAPTER SIXTY-NINE

1981

We have reached the breaking point, losing all optimism of a possible resolution to the war. Countless times we have been forced out of our home and out of the country and yet we somehow maintained our naive faith that things will return to normal, coming back, rebuilding and waiting.

Since the beginning of this war, our love and dedication for our country has been met by a violent and deadly outcome. It was time to sever the ties and move on with our lives. Our only salvation was to accept the sad truth that the fate of our country was in the hands of national and international players who controlled their followers on the ground like pawns in a chess game, unyielding to one another until someone declares a checkmate.

Our US visas were still valid and could be used at anytime. Once again, we had to rid ourselves of all our material possessions including all the furniture, kitchen ware, electronics, cars and clothing we had purchase since returning. This time however, we were only renting our apartment so the pressure of selling was not there.

Not so for my Uncle and grandmother who had bought their apartment and were faced with the decision to sell, lease or just leave everything behind as is.

My uncle had not forgotten his previous attempt to settle in the US and how much he hated it. Thus, he decided that he should just lock up the apartment with everything in it and leave. My mother's sister, aunt Wadad, lived in the next building to my uncle and was entrusted with the apartment in their absence.

We gave away most of our belongings, dividing everything equally between my mother's three sisters and her brother. The living room furniture went to her brother, the bedrooms to one sister, electronics to another and wall paintings and kitchen to another.

Only a month earlier my uncle had bought me a state of the art Sharp stereo system, which I sadly had to give to our upstairs neighbor. All we were left with was our clothes, which we packed into suitcases and awaited the opening of the airport. By the end of June, 1981 the airport was partially opened and we prepared to leave for the US. My dad had wired uncle Eddy in Philadelphia informing him of the date of our arrival so that he could pick us up from the airport. Our travel route was Beirut, London, then Philadelphia.

Along with his apartment, my uncle decided to keep his Volvo car behind and entrusted my aunt's husband with it in his absence. The day before our last, I asked my uncle to take me on a short ride to a special place, which I wanted to visit for the last time before leaving, and he agreed to do so.

The Burning Cedars

RAMZY BAROODY

CHAPTER SEVENTY

THE BURNT REMAINS OF A CEDAR TREE

As we prepared to leave the country again, I had the feeling that this time things would be different. In my heart I wished for the war to end and for us to be able to return and settle down indefinitely, but the reality of the situation, what I was seeing and hearing, was telling a different story.

Lebanon was like a bubbling cauldron on an open fire, filled to capacity with many diverse and contradictory ingredients, churning and interacting violently until reaching the boiling point, at which time they spilled over wildly out of control, injuring and burning everyone and everything in their path. I saw, with deep sadness and despair, the profound hatred, the unquenched desire to kill and dominate, the unquestioned "divine" orders to destroy all who think and act differently and those who believe in a different God who, in the name of God, are themselves killing and pillaging.

While on the surface this may have appeared to be a "holy war," the underlying reality was much more complex and secular:

The Burning Cedars

JUSTIFIED KILLING IN THE NAME OF.........

Money Oil Greed

US Russia Power

Egos Control Influence

Food Crops Bekaa-Valey

Guns Drugs Rewards

Interventions Syria Israel

Christians Muslims Druze

Jews Palestinians Arabs

Profits Prophets Prophecies

RAMZY BAROODY

On July 24, 1981, the day before we were scheduled to leave, I wanted to take one final trip to a place which meant so much to me growing up. I wanted to visit my old school, Beirut Evangelical.

For me, that place epitomized growing up in Lebanon; my uncomfortable and lonely youth, my interaction with people from other countries who spoke and taught in a different language, my teachers who taught and empathized me for my socially awkward disposition, my dad's show of strength and love, my brother's disappearing acts, my caring yet childless taxi driver who adopted me as his son, my Christmas performances which my parents never saw, my noontime hideaway under the olive trees and my witnessing the start of the civil war from my classroom window back in 1975.

My uncle agreed to take me for one last goodbye and on that day in 1981, on an unusually quiet and hot July afternoon, we made the trip. It was eerily quiet and the roads empty with the exception of the occasional checkpoint where soldiers sat lazily behind their sandbags casually waving the occasional car through.

We arrived at the school and the first thing I noticed was that the exterior walls looked like a piece of Swiss cheese, scarred with numerous holes from gunfire and shrapnel hits. As we pulled into the driveway, there were children playing in the front yard, which was now overgrown with weeds and small trees. On the balconies overlooking the playgrounds hung articles of laundry, placed there in the sun to dry. We realized that many families had taken refuge in the school and made it their home. As we exited the car an elderly man inquiring as to our intentions for being there approached us. He spoke with a Palestinian accent and we knew that these families were

The Burning Cedars

Palestinian refugees driven out of Southern Lebanon by the Israeli Invasions. My uncle explained to the man that I had gone to school there a few years back and we just wanted to look around. The man looked at me and without saying a word, motioned for us to walk by. We walked up to the second floor and down the main corridor passing by classrooms full of people going about their daily business.

In one, an elderly woman was hunched over a metal basin hand washing clothes as beads of sweat dripped off her forehead into the mucky soapy water. Although it was a hot July day, the woman was dressed in a heavy torn sweater and an equally shabby long colorful skirt as she sat on a plastic milk container on the floor.

In the next room, the family had gathered around an open fire they had built in the middle of the floor where they were cooking their dinner.

Children with torn and filthy clothes ran up and down the corridors playing hide and seek then coming up to us asking our names and if we were looking for someone.

I told my uncle that I have seen enough and we headed towards the church building. Inside, people had turned the main hall into a gathering place where dozens of families were hanging out, sleeping, eating or bathing. The walls were charred black with the smoke of the wood burning pits scattered around the hall, used for cooking and warming bath water.

It was a sad and unreal sight to see my beautiful school turned into such a chaotic and medieval-looking place, but in this time of war, people had to do whatever they could to survive. Before returning to the car, I told my uncle that there is still one place I'd like to visit before leaving. I took him by the hand and we walked to the garden in the back of the church.

Stepping over broken bottles, discarded bags and empty bullet shells, we turned the corner around the back and there, in the center of the garden, in the midst of piles of garbage and discarded old clothing, stood the remnant of a burnt cedar tree.

Mr. white, the school principal, had planted this tree many years earlier during the end of the school year dedication ceremony as a symbol of the resilience and beauty of my country.

Now all that remained was the burnt cedar tree stem peeking cruelly from among the ashes and the garbage carelessly discarded there by those who neither appreciated nor cared for what this tree symbolizes to so many.

It was ironic that the same people who initiated and were behind the war should burn one of the most adored and regarded symbols of the country which houses and feeds them.

As we stood there looking at this heartbreaking sight in disbelief, tears rolled down my cheeks and when my uncle saw this, he gently took my hand and we walked away.

Neither of us said a word as we drove back home and every once in a while, my uncle would turn and look at me with sadness and understanding as I sat there trying to fully comprehend the implications of what I had just witnessed.

The Burning Cedars

This day marked the end of so many things. It was a kind of a closure to things that were, things that are and the beginning of many things that will soon come to fruition. Good and bad things beyond what anyone could have imagined at the time. Things that awaited us as we embarked on a new journey to a new country.

In 1981, the promise of leaving everything behind for a new life seemed unimaginably appealing and exciting. Yet in life, nothing or no one is perfect.

Our new life would be reminiscent of a bible passage which accurately portrays the toils and tribulations of human existence and which accurately describes our adventure as we struggle to establish a new life as refugees ourselves in a new country.

RAMZY BAROODY

AS IF A MAN DID FLEE FROM A LION,
AND A BEAR MET HIM;
OR WENT INTO THE HOUSE,
AND LEANED HIS HAND ON THE WALL,
AND A SERPENT BIT HIM.

AMOS 5:19

www.ingramcontent.com/pod-product-compliance
Lightning Source LLC
Chambersburg PA
CBHW022353040426
42450CB00005B/163